THE ESSENTIAL
DICK GREGORY

ALSO BY DICK GREGORY

THE ESSENTIAL
DICK GREGORY

DICK GREGORY

EDITED BY
CHRISTIAN GREGORY

AMISTAD

An Imprint of HarperCollins*Publishers*

HarperCollins books may be purchased for educational, business, or sales promotional use. For information, please email the Special Markets Department at SPsales@harpercollins.com.

Photograph by Chris Felver/Getty Images

FIRST EDITION

Library of Congress Cataloging-in-Publication Data has been applied for.

ISBN 978-0-06-287920-2

22 23 24 25 26   FRI   10 9 8 7 6 5 4 3 2 1

To Lil

CONTENTS

PART III: THE SPIRIT (1971–2017)

FOREWORD

Separated by almost exactly one century, two significant events were responsible for capturing the minds of Americans and creating the man we would all come to know as the one and only Dick Gregory. The first was the raid on Harpers Ferry by famed abolitionist John Brown in October 1859, which was often called the dress rehearsal or tragic prelude to the American Civil War. The second was the publishing of a remarkable article in *Ebony* magazine in October 1960 entitled "Why Negro Comics Don't Make It Big," in which Dick Gregory was mentioned for the first time on the national stage as a mere "newcomer."

To most historians, comedians, and students of the Black experience in America, these events appear to represent two fundamentally unrelated circumstances in the shaping of our country as we know it. However, every year on Dick Gregory's birthday, a date which almost perfectly aligns with John Brown's October raid, Dick Gregory would visit Harpers Ferry in memoriam. On every second of December, he would go to Charles Town, Virginia (now in West Virginia), and hug the tree where John Brown was hanged. "I hug the tree for the white man who gave up his life for the Black man," he said. "There are trees all over the world. Lots of other places have trees. What they do not have that [this] tree has is [the spirit] of John Brown." Without the historic raid on Harpers Ferry, without the death of John Brown and the end of the enslavement of Black people in America, we might not have ever heard the name Dick Gregory or seen it introduced to the world in that *Ebony* article one century later.

Everyone knows that the 1960s were a tumultuous time in our nation's history, but few people know that even comedy itself was segregated between Blacks and whites. In that same *Ebony* article, one white club owner would say, "I am very apprehensive about booking Negroes into my club. I don't want a Negro comedian entertaining whites at the expense of Negro people." The famed television star Steve Allen even more poignantly stated, "One reason that there is a shortage of Negro stand-up comedians or humorists is that comedy of this sort usually involves a certain amount of critical observation and our society is probably not civilized enough yet to permit or encourage the Negro comedian to make satirical commentary about Eisenhower's golf game, our bungled international relations, the Un-American Activities Committee or other things of that sort." Steve Allen would go on to conclude, "Just imagine a Negro comic getting up on stage and saying some of the things that Lenny Bruce or Mort Sahl are getting away with."

Barely three months after the publication of this story, Dick Gregory, the so-called "newcomer," would prove Steve Allen wrong—or right, depending on your point of view—and wrap all of the prejudicial conjecture, race theory, and misfired predictions of critics and TV stars into the palm of his hand, then take the mic on the biggest stage possible in those days, *The Jack Paar Show* on NBC.

At the outset of my six-year journey to bring the incredible life story of Dick Gregory to film, I was vastly unaware of the immense complexity behind Dick Gregory's brand of humor. Throughout his life, Dick Gregory was often made an example of, sometimes by his own design; Black folks projected our woes onto him, and white folks cherished—or reviled—him for shining a mirror on their own prejudice.

For me, the personal experiences of Dick Gregory were like listening to a walking history lesson. It took only a few hours into my journey to make this film for me to realize that Dick Gregory was one of a kind, and I became totally consumed. In 1975, Dick Gregory quit comedy, staging his last nightclub performance at Paul's Mall in Boston, Massachusetts. The announcer who introduced Dick Gregory read a letter from his publicist, Steve Jaffe, that highlighted the power of his contributions to society. One passage went like this: "No man has given more, asked less, or been more needed." Albeit only a brief summation of the gifts of Dick Gregory, I can think of no more prescient a phrase to describe what he would come to mean to the world.

Dick Gregory is often credited as being a *civil rights* activist, and although it may have started that way, civil rights, like comedy, was never his terminus. Yes, he was an activist, but more appropriately, he was an advocate and protector of *human rights*. Thus when the time came to create a graphic for the poster to represent the film, none was more fitting than that of Dick Gregory, sitting center stage, illuminated by infinite silhouettes of himself in the different colors of the rainbow. The array of colors represents to me not only the many lives that Dick Gregory lived but also his aura. While he walked the Earth as a Black man, talked and thought as a Black man, he could *feel* like everyman, and his spirit, heart, and empathy toward all mankind are what made him the great teacher, guru, adviser, and friend he became to me and the world. When you combine all of those colors together, it produces the white light as projected by the sun, and no one better understood the power of the sun, or how to use it as a force of good and righteousness, than Dick Gregory.

—Andre Gaines, producer and director,
The One and Only Dick Gregory

LETTER FROM THE EDITOR

What a life, what a blessing. Dick Gregory was many things—he metamorphosed from athlete to comedian to activist to presidential candidate to nutritionist to social critic—at no point leaving behind the nucleus holding him together: love. Love—love for self, love for thy neighbor, love for humankind, love for nature—was the engine that powered his many manifestations.

Metamorphosis is a change of the form or nature of a thing or person into a completely different one, by natural or supernatural means. It's typically brought about by both internal and external forces. The sum of these forces produces a new manifestation that advances its previous form. At every iteration, Dick Gregory was passionate about life, laughter, and equality. There was not a righteous movement in his lifetime that his blood, sweat, or tears didn't impact—his activism was rooted in love and dignity.

Richard Claxton Gregory's life was incredibly well-lived. My colleagues and I studied his mind like the science it often was. We've extrapolated from his lifetime the building blocks and experiences that help explain his unyielding life of service. Generations will delve into his sacrifice, comedic genius, focus, and aptitude. Civil rights, women's rights, children's rights, human rights, disabled rights, animal rights . . . Dick Gregory's DNA is on virtually every movement for fairness and equality for all livings things on this planet. He taught us the power of love by example.

Dick Gregory was always busy but never hurried. He made time for everyone and almost everything. He wrote a lot but talked more. He left us so much to pore over, including sixteen books, twelve albums, hundreds of interviews and syndicated news columns, and hundreds of hours of archival footage. The challenge we faced was whittling down this extraordinary amount of material to present in a succinct structure.

We were able to organize this book into three primary sections— "The Body" (covering his early life from 1932 to 1960), "The Mind" (discourse related to his early career, from 1961 to 1970), and "The Spirit" (later career thoughts and work from 1971 to 2017)—to highlight the periods in his life where his aptitude and brilliance evolved. With the exception of the headnotes, which provide orientation and historical positioning, everything was written or said by Dick Gregory in his own unique style, tempo, and cadence.

The highlights of Dick Gregory's life are well known. However, the ebbs and flows were lost in the brightness of the peaks. More often than not, the real lessons are in the journey. I'm delighted to have you take this journey with us. I trust you'll be as uplifted and inspired as we were cultivating and compiling this collection.

Loving and lovable,

CHRISTIAN CLAXTON GREGORY

PART I

THE BODY

(1932–1960)

On October 12, 1932, state file number 124–32–045154 was issued to one Richard Claxton Gregory, the second son of mother Lucille Franklin (twenty-eight) of Missouri and father Presley Gregory (thirty-four) of Tennessee. The first decade of life was about to be profoundly difficult for Richard, who would experience the Great Depression and Jim Crow. The skinniest kid on the block in the Ville would also be the poorest. Black Tuesday's thick, black smoke from coal-burning emissions would turn seven-year-old Richard's days into the darkest of nights. Lurking in all that darkness was a spirit so full of promise that a psychic acknowledged a star on his head. Stars are not born; they are formed, a perfect combination of nature and nurture. Pressure and heat make steel; sustained pressure on coal yields diamonds. This diamond in the rough would go on to shine so brightly that he would be a light bearer, using his light to leave the world better than he found it.

—CHRISTIAN GREGORY

1803 NORTH TAYLOR

ALL RAMPS, NO STAIRS

I was malnourished. As a matter of fact, I was so small that they sent me to a special school in St. Louis called Turner Open Air School. This was where disabled kids went, or kids that had polio or were handicapped, kids with one leg or with one arm, or with very bad eyes or who were underweight. I guess I went there for a year, or maybe a little bit longer. Kids used to harass me a lot because to go to that school meant something was wrong with you.

I was very young. I guess I was seven or eight. The school district authorities would just come like the dogcatchers and pick you up out of public school. Just barely short of the hook and the net, and catch you and grab you, and put you in there. But I dug the school myself. I mean, people used to put it down and say there was something wrong with me, and this and that. But we were the few kids that had a bus come by to pick me and my brother up every morning. We got on the bus, went to school, ate, and had a rest period with real clean beds. You brushed your teeth there; you combed your hair. I learned a lot from that school. Got food and filtered air! I don't know anybody else in public school in America that had filtered air. Maybe this is the reason that my lungs developed so strong was from the filtered air, and eventually led to me being a great trackman.

I don't know what the reason was, but we left and went back to public school.

There was one time I think I stayed out of public school for three months or six months when my feet were frostbitten when I was out selling papers. Little kid, nine or ten years old. I came home, stuck my feet right in the oven, and they swelled up like a balloon and split right down the middle. I couldn't go to school then and consequently, I was like fifteen years old before I finished grade school, and twenty years old before I finished high school.

THE VALUE OF HUMOR IN HIS CHILDHOOD

Kids used to pick on me a lot. They would tell me I didn't have a daddy. Tell me I was on relief. I used to get mad and run home. And I think that's when I first began to find out about humor. I didn't know at the time. I found out if a guy starts talking about you and the crowd starts laughing with him, there's nothing you can do or say. And I knew some of the things I was saying were much funnier than the things they were saying about me, but I never knew why they would laugh.

I laid home in bed one night and I figured it out. I haven't got 'em with me. I'm the skinniest kid on the block. My daddy's not home; they know I'm on relief. Can I get 'em with me? So I used to come out, and when I'd see 'em coming, I'd start talking about myself. I started making jokes about me not having no daddy, making jokes about how hard my mother worked, how poor we were. I don't remember now, but I said some pretty funny things. I mean, things like the shoes they had on fit them a little better than mine, but the shoes I had on cost more than theirs did because the white folks sent my shoes to me. And I knew I had me a good pair of shoes on. The shirt might have been a little big, but it was a good shirt.

I knew the people my mother was working for would go to Africa and go hunting. So at seven and eight years old, I was one of the few kids in America, let alone Black, that knew what bear meat tasted like because Mama cooked it for the white folks and brought it home. It was amusing to me to think I'm one of the few kids in America that ever tasted bear meat, as poor as I was, and had nerve enough not to like it. Here's a man, goes all the way to Africa to take a chance on losing his life and be away from his family and loved ones. Caught his game and brought it home, and little poor me on relief didn't like it. And I used to wonder how many times, how many guys would take a chance on going to jail just to steal some bear meat. I was one of the few kids on the block that knew what champagne tastes like 'cause they'd give me champagne. Sometimes Mama'd bring it home and we'd taste it. I was one of the few kids on the block who knew what caviar tastes like, 'cause the white folks she was working for would give her caviar, and sometimes she'd bring it home. Didn't like champagne. Didn't like caviar. I didn't like bear meat. So I had a lot of things, personally, that were funny to me.

Once I started talking about myself for fifteen or twenty minutes, I could turn and pick them out one at a time and talk about them. Told them their daddy was coming home drunk. Told them their mother was running up a bigger charge account with Mr. Ben [the white neighborhood grocer] than we were. Told them about the Christmas we used to have in July when the white folks would give my mother toys in the middle of the summer and Mama would bring them home to us. I had many things I could talk about, and I noticed that once you get a man laughing with you, it's hard for him to laugh at you. The whole thing changed then.

Then, with my little skinny, underweight self, it got to the point that the big boys would run when they would see me coming.

'Cause before I'd say hello, I'd ask them, "How's your mammy? How's your drunken, no-good daddy?" And I could show 'em my daddy not being at home, but when his daddy was at home, I could raise my window at night and hear him whipping his mother. Tell him, "Sleep with your window open and see if you hear any noises coming out of my house. With no daddy in my house, we still have peace." They'd laugh because I'd pick one out and do it to the one it was happening to. And then I'd look at another one and say the police wagon has never pulled up to my house to get none of Miss Gregory's sons. They came by my house last night and asked me for your number, and I gave it to 'em.

So I began to find out how humor played. And from that point on, I always used it.

I'd even used it with myself. One time I broke my arm, and I couldn't cry for thinking about how funny it was with those run-down heels on my shoes, that if the heels would have been right when I turned that corner, I wouldn't have slipped, and my arm wouldn't have been broken. Well, it's funny to me because a worn-out heel could break an arm, but I don't know any arm that could break a heel. There was a lot of humor we would find twenty-four hours a day.

FINDING HIS WAY IN SCHOOL

If they couldn't mark me on my ability to get along in a crowd, neatness, and politeness, I guess I would have flunked everything.

I had certain qualities that overshadowed. The ability to be able to talk, the ability to stand up and ad-lib on something I didn't know. (I'd take an hour to explain it to the teacher, why I didn't know it.) I didn't have to read the book. If the teacher called on anyone and gave this kid a question, if the kid answered it right, I would literally sit and try to tear a hole in the whole structure of why this should be like this. I remember one time I stood up in math, and I said, "If two and two is four, then actually all you're really saying is that it takes two, two times, to be subtracted before you can get zero. You'd have to subtract two from four two times to get zero." I used to hang the class up in this way. And I used to literally sit and try to find a myth, try to find a crack through, try to break down everything that was said. If the teacher said, "You're right. You're very right," then I would raise my hand and I would want to push it to an nth degree further to find out, well why is this right? Why did this happen this way? Who were the other people that had something to do with the Constitution of the United States?

I knew there was more to these things than what was brought out on the surface. I just knew this. I don't know why.

It would make an impression on me when I got to stand up and find some kind of flaw in a book, not even by reading it, but by hearing kids get up and say what they had read and then hear the teacher express what they said was right. It was my job to go knock a hole in the whole theory.

At this period in my life, I was the guy who would always break up the fight. If I heard there was a fight going on anywhere in the school, I would run out of class to break it up.

I didn't care how big or small they were. With the big guy picking on the little guy, I would go and break up the fight. I'd be scared to death. The big guy usually threatened to whup me, but I would always be able to negotiate. I used to look to the back of the class, at the kids who used to sit where I used to sit in the "idiot seat," and say, "Man, why don't you shut up?" And then they'd slip me a note and say they were going to beat me up after class was over. I'd definitely be scared, but I knew between the time class was up, school was out, and the time this had happened, I'd be able to go back and negotiate some kind of way. Which I always did, and never did I ever have them as much as grab me.

I WAS GOING TO BE SOMEBODY

I was hungry so much that when I got full, it felt strange. Hunger was my best friend. We walked together, talked together, we ate together. Just seemed like me and hunger got hungry together. Stayed weak a lot, but I didn't realize what it was. I wasn't eating good meals. I got candy from the store with the money I made hustling, selling newspapers. A lot of times they'd beat me up and take my paper money from me. I go back to the guy where I had to check in my money, and he'd cheat me out of some money.

For some reason or another, I always seemed to have the best route in anything I wanted because I was so nice to people. And I knew how to smile.

I was going to be somebody. I was going somewhere. I used to feel like a man feels when he's just thirsty enough to want a drink, not thirsty enough to die from not getting it.

My mother always told me there's something about you, the way you walk, the way you talk, that makes me think you're something different. I used to tell her no because even when she told me that, she couldn't say it as strongly as I felt it. That's why I never did anything to go to jail because I knew I was going somewhere. I didn't know where, but I knew I was going. She used to always tell us, "Just walk that straight path." On that straight path, you will meet men, and when you meet a man, pick him up gently and pull him clean, then never hang around to hear him say how he still would have been in the gutter had you not reached for him. Because you don't need this. Pull him clean, so he might reach and pull another.

If he's so busy telling you thanks, he might not see those other men laying down there.

SHE WAS THAT PICTURE OF GOD

When she was around, that sweetness was there, and that shadow she left when she was gone, there was no way you could get around it. Mom was there twenty-four hours a day. I've had a whole lot of people offer me a whole lot of money not to say some of the things that I say. It never even bothered me. I hear people make the statement that everybody has a price. I just go along with them and say yeah.

But my mother did not have a price. She couldn't be bought. Not to think I'm half as good as Mom was, but it would be real funny for me to find out what my price would be. I won't say just yet that I haven't got one.

My mother had pictures of the Ten Commandments, pictures of God on the wall, which we very seldom had to even look at because she portrayed them in herself. She was the Ten Commandments. She was that picture of God. And the reason I didn't go wrong was that she kept me strong enough, looking at her until I could crack some books and see some other great people.

Used to hear people talk about Mrs. Roosevelt. I used to say, "Boy, if Mrs. Roosevelt knew Mama, she'd be talking about Mama." She was the champ. Yep, there was something about that woman, when we had no food at all, she could strengthen us where we were weak, and build us up where we're torn down by just talking to us.

POWER OF LAUGHTER

You've bought and paid for what has happened to you. You want to sit down and give a man for free what you bought and paid for?

Good. But don't let him take it. If you walk through life showing the aggravation you've gone through, another man could see that and feel sorry for you. No man can respect a man he feels sorry for.

For some reason, you can get closer to the whole world with a smile. Twenty-four hours a day my mother smiled—to the extent it was molded on her face. Never showed nobody nothing. Sometimes I believe she tried to hide it from herself. Nobody knew.

A man has always had two ways out in life: laughing or crying. Mother taught us that there is more hope in laughing than there is in crying. A man who falls down the steps can lay there in such horror that his wife will collapse and faint. But if he can just hold back his pain for a few minutes, she might collect herself enough to go and call the doctor and ambulance, and it might mean the difference between him living and being able to laugh again, or dying right there on the spot.

POVERTY AND BEING ON RELIEF

I was the most sensitive kid in class. I was the one with the most sense because I had enough to know there was something wrong with the world. I didn't know what was wrong with it, but I knew at the age of seven years old something had to happen. Somebody had to straighten it out. You know, Mom used to always tell us that we were not poor. I didn't understand what she meant 'til I came home one day and finally got enough nerve to tell her what the teacher had said. And Mom sat me down on her lap. She told me, "Son, you're not poor; you're just broke. To be poor is a mental condition. To be broke is a temporary situation. One you can grow out of; another you can never grow out of."

She wanted to get off relief. I guess at certain times she was able to see the embarrassment I was going through being on relief. She decided she would sell lunches. She cooked the food at home and then put it in baskets and took it out to various hotels and places where there'd be people working that had a lunch break at a certain time.

Construction work. Factories. Mainly she'd go to hotels. The maids, the porters, the bellhops. Many people would come out to the back where she would sell lunches and buy them. She tried this for a long period of time, and I think it would have worked, but she got too sick. She got to the point where she couldn't keep this up.

I don't know why, but it was a very embarrassing thing when I had to take these baskets with her and get on the streetcar. You could smell this food—fish, chicken, and all of this. I was embarrassed when the streetcar conductor started buying his lunch from her. I mean, we had to get on the streetcar with these baskets of food, and she would stop right there and open it up, take a spoon and stick it in spaghetti and the fish, and give it to a conductor. This embarrassed me to no end. I knew it was honest. I knew it was clean. I knew it was legit, but for some reason down the line, I just didn't want to see Mama with these baskets. Because you want to see your mother, anything she does, doing it the most sophisticated way. And I figured if she had a restaurant, this was the most sophisticated way. But when she had to put it in baskets and take it out . . . I don't know. This just hurt me, and I resented it a whole lot.

MOTHER'S LESSONS

My mother was the proudest woman in St. Louis.

All she did was brought us the best she could bring us. She used to always tell us, "Do what you want to do, and you'll never get cheated. Work hard at what you believe in, and you'll be admired by kings." I tried to scrub better steps than anybody, tried to sell more papers than anybody, tried to be more honest than anybody when I was making negotiations for a sale, selling newspapers, or shining shoes.

Shoe shining was an interesting thing in my life because I came in contact with people when they were happy in the taverns, sitting around talking, arguing. I never will forget I was in a white tavern one time. Everybody was calling me "shine" and "moonlight." Called me "gorilla," "monkey." I just kept shining. Every now and then a white man would rub my head. I kind of thought he liked me, it was like saying, "Hi, son." 'Til one day a white man rubbed my head and gave me a $20 bill. I walked home and asked my mother, "Mama, white people been rubbing my head for years, a white man rubbed my head today and he gave me $20, Mama. Why?" She sat down and she explained, "They rub a Negro's head because they think he's lucky."

I burned the $20 bill up. Bought myself an ice pick and I put it in my shoeshine stand. The next time I was on my knees shining a white man's shoes, and he reached down and rubbed my head, I got my ice pick out. When I saw his hand, I stabbed at it—not knowing his hand wasn't even on my head—and stabbed myself in the head. Matter of fact, I still carry the spot where the ice pick stuck me.

Every time a white man would rub my head, I'd duck out from underneath him.

I kept shining shoes. Never will forget I was in the tavern one Saturday afternoon, one of the women was wearing brown and white shoes. I was a little kid, maybe close to nine, but I looked like I was seven because I was so small. I was shining this white woman's shoes and I didn't want to get the white polish on her stockings, so to steady yourself, you put your other hand behind the leg. They'd been sitting there drinking beer and calling me a bunch of dirty names. They asked this woman, "Is that your boyfriend?" Laughing and playing. She made a couple dirty remarks, and a white man sitting next to her (that had never looked around the whole time) turned around, kicked me in my mouth, and said, "Get your hand off that white woman's leg!" Broke my teeth out. Busted my lip.

I didn't even know he'd done all this because I looked around and the fight was on. They were fighting one another. The bartender jumped over the counter, beat up a couple of guys, and grabbed me and my shoeshine box. On the way out, he said, "I'm sorry, boy." He reached into his pocket and gave me $20. The only thing I could think of was, "Gee, if I can get kicked in my mouth twenty more times, I'd have a good day." That always bothered me. I sit there not doing anything wrong. A man kicked me in the mouth after everybody had been playing with me, these same people that have been laughing and joking with me and insulting me. They jumped up and beat him up.

The bartender walked me outside, said he was sorry, but told me to never come back in there. It took me almost twenty years to figure it out, but I never forgot it. These white folks were laughing and joking with a little nigger, but when this guy kicked me in my mouth, he kicked a kid. That's when I became a kid to these white men. And they jumped on him to beat him up.

The bartender was in there trying to make him a living. He paid me the $20 for the man being wrong, but he couldn't afford to have his customers fighting over me in his tavern. I learned a hell of a lesson from that because it also played a very important part in my entertainment career.

FAITH AND WISDOM

I believed everything Mom told us. We had our moments, but you understood her goodness, understood her kindness.

When she got on her knees to say a prayer, you felt like God was really in that room. I used to slip up to her sometimes and ask her to ask him for something for me. For some reason or another, I knew he heard her. I'd seen too many things Mom would ask for that, the next week, she'd get them. I've seen her fall on her knees and pray that the lights would be turned back on. Saw the man come by, turn the lights on. Seen her fall on her knees and pray for some coal because the kids were sick and needed heat in the house. The health inspector came and looked down in the basement and condemned the basement, it was so filthy down there. The pipes had busted, water running all over everything. The police came by that night because this white health inspector saw the conditions, knew he was talking to a real woman, went by the police department, and left money for a ton of coal. Police come by that night to leave the coal for her. She was short, but she seemed like she was twenty feet tall.

She's the type of woman you would never put in a contest. She was the type of woman, when people start talking about Miss America, you automatically knew they won second best, 'cause Mom was Miss America. And as I grew up, I realized it was an honor just knowing this woman, let alone having her as my mother. White men and Black men used to come here crying, telling her their problems. All types of white men. Sometimes white men where she worked, sometimes white men that she had met in passing. The bums and the tramps, the doctors and schoolteachers used to come by and talk to Mom. Politicians would come by to get advice, wisdom. She had it. She had a way she could talk to people. Heard a man come by the house that was getting ready to go kill somebody. When he finished talking to Mom, the man left crying and thanked her. A white man thinking of committing suicide came by, talked to Mom. She had a quality that was second only to God. She had a quality where she could sit by, in all her misery and all her suffering, she could sit by and evaluate the situation, evaluate a problem, tell a man things. I used to look at her tell people things they didn't even want to hear because they were coming to get her to okay the cheap way out. After they finished explaining why she had to do a certain thing, she still won them over.

Had a lot of people come by who thought she was a good touch. Used to hear them telling her, how could she live there, raising all those boys without a father? Used to hear men come by the house and offer her money. Never took it. Used to hear them come by and tell her how much they admired her. Used to hear her tell them, "Anytime you want to come by the house and talk, you can come by. You can never come by this house and flirt with me because I've got too many boys I've got to raise. If people see you coming in here, they'll think you're doing something wrong."

I heard a guy say, "I wanted to come here just to talk to you, Mrs. Gregory. People will think I'm coming in to have an affair with you." My mother used to say, as long as my boys know nothing is going on with no man, and as long as I know, nothing else counts. And as many men used to come in my house to seek advice, not one time did I hear a kid saying anything smutty about my mother. It was a funny thing. Even the bill collector called her Miss Lucille. Even the kids in the neighborhood always referred to Mom as Miss Gregory.

White folks used her as a social symbol. If a white home had Mrs. Gregory around for a cocktail party, it was probably one of the greatest cocktail parties of the year. And poor white folks used to get mom to come by their house. Mom used to charge them $20 a day. Hated 'em. Not because they were white, because they were white and so poor and so low-down. No class. Used to come home and tell us about them. Things they'd try to do. How they used to treat her because they think this is the way rich people are supposed to treat a Black woman. Call her nigger. Call her girl. Make her do a whole lot of dirty work. Make her lift things.

Used to hurt Mom when she had to wash a white man's underwear, white woman's drawers, and they were dirtier than hers. She knew rich people changed their underwear every day. Rich people's sheets were easy to wash. Mom could just walk in a house and look at the man's socks and know where he was. Knew how long he'd been rich, and knew almost how long he was gonna stay rich. One day she came home, she's really broken up, crying because of this white man she was working for that morning. The same pot he was washing his feet in, he wanted her to cook spaghetti in it that evening. She walked out. Came home and told me how low-down they were.

In a Black home, after they wash the clothes on the board, they boiled them out on the stove. Put them on a stove and put the bleach in it. That's why a Black woman always was proud about having the whitest wash. Because after she washed the clothes with her hands, she rinsed them out in the kitchen sink, put them in the dishpan, and boiled them. Put the laundry stick in the pan, boiled 'em, boiled 'em, boiled 'em, then rinsed the bleach out of them and then hung them on the line. I asked Mom when she came home crying about that man soaking his feet in the pot, "What difference does it make if a man soaks his feet in the pot that you cook spaghetti in?" Mom looked at me and told me, "I didn't know I was raising a son that low-down. You can't see nothing wrong with that?" I said, "Hell no, Mama, I can't see anything wrong with it. Not when I sit up and watch you wash the clothes, then boil our drawers out in the same pan we wash dishes in." She didn't answer, but I noticed she went out and bought a bucket for our clothes.

BIG PRES

"Richard, you know, your daddy's a cook. He has to work on Christmas."

I said, "He'll be here, Mom."

She went back and put her clothes on. She was very nervous. She came back and asked me how she looked. I said, "You look okay, Mom."

She said, "The best pair of shoes I have back there, Miss Wallace gave them to me, but they're summer shoes."

"What do you mean by 'summer shoes,' Mama? Those black and white shoes, the ones I like so much, the ones you never wear because you never have no place to go? I didn't know those were summer shoes."

"You never see people wearing them in the wintertime."

"No, Mom, they dye them."

"They dye 'em?"

"Yeah, I dye 'em for people."

I went in the kitchen, and I got my dye out. She walked out and said, "What are you doing?" I said, "I'm dying your shoes. So you could put them on. So Daddy can see you in these."

She said, "Oh, you can't put that on. They have to dry first."

"Oh, Mom, you burn it. You burn it, and it dries while you're putting it on."

"Really, Richard?"

"Yeah, Mom."

We sat and looked out the window together. Four o'clock in the morning.

"Guess I didn't have to burn them, did I?"

"You didn't have to burn them, but I'm glad you did. Never really believed he was coming. Why do you believe he's coming, Richard?"

"I talked to that man in the backyard. I thought he was. Guess he's not coming now."

"Go to bed, Richard."

"No, Mom, I'll wait here with you. If I lay over there in a chair, when he comes, would you wake me up?"

"Yeah, Richard. Get you some sleep. No little boy stays up this late."

"Okay, Mom."

That's a horrible feeling, to lay in a chair trying to sleep, and can't sleep because Mama thinks you're asleep. And for the first time, you hear Mom praying. Not the type of prayers she usually says when she knows the kids are here. I never will forget how she said it.

"God, I've always made a big mistake. I've sat here every Christmas, many times in the summer, and prayed for their daddy and never prayed for the other kids' daddies that are on their way home too. Send them theirs first, and then, if you're not too tired and weary, oh Lord, send Big Pres here. And when you send him, don't send him for me. Send him because the boys need him."

And then she fell out on the floor and cried.

It's a funny feeling to be hugging your mother while you're a kid, and she's crying, and you're telling her don't cry. She cried, and she cried, and she cried. Until she cried herself to sleep. Then I turned the tree off, and I sat in the chair and I looked at her. I said, "God, wherever he is, let him knock on the door. I'll wait for him."

You know, with all the odds that the man wasn't coming, it

was always a funny thing when I was a kid and would pray. Never prayed that much, not real prayers. I always prayed social prayers. It was nice to pray before you go to bed because it made Mom happy. But I never really prayed for something that I didn't get.

I never will forget it. My aunt knocked on the door and said, "Let me speak to your mother."

I thought she was daddy knocking, and I could tell the way she looked at me that in some kind of way, he did knock. My aunt woke her up. We had always been trained to leave when a grown person comes into the room. I heard my aunt tell my mother, "Big Pres been by my house all night. He's scared to come home because he hasn't got anything for the kids but some money. Just got in this evening. Been over there crying, 'Cille, all day because he went and gambled. And won. But when he finished winning, all the stores were closed."

I was so happy I ran in and said, "I told you, didn't I, Mama? I told you he was coming! Go get him, Mom, and tell him we got everything we want."

She went to get him, and I woke up all the kids and told them Daddy's home. They flipped out of bed.

We sat there and we waited. We looked out the window and we waited. And Dolores said, "Oh, he's not here. I don't want to see him anyway."

Ronald said, "I do."

We started betting what he would look like.

"Oh, man, he'd be clean!"

"Two-hundred-dollar suit on!"

Presley said, "Daddy wears $1,000 suits!"

Garland said, "He'd have a pocketful of money too!"

I said to myself, "Yep. Pocketful of money, but no gifts."

Cab pulled up. We heard the door slam. And I heard a big deep voice like nobody but my daddy could say it: "Keep the change."

We hollered, we screamed, we jumped up and down. The last thing I remember was taking that last look over my shoulders at my brothers and sisters, fighting each other to get to the door. And hearing my mother say, "Don't touch his clothes."

Yeah, because he used to bitch a lot when we used to crawl up on him with our dirty selves. I used to hear him telling her about "those dirty brats." Yeah, that's the last thing I remember before I slammed the door to my bedroom. It was *my* bedroom that night, 'cause everybody was gone. And I crawled up in that bed and I got real frightened, laying there crying. Hearing him talk to the kids. Hearing him saying, "Where's Richard?" Hearing my mother call me: "Richard! Big Pres is here!" And scared for him to come see what I was doing, for fear he might walk out that door like he's walked out so many other times when her back was turned.

I laid there and I remembered how that bed has always been a happy bed. We had a lot of fun in bed. But not tonight. It's the loneliest bed in the world. Because the one thing I resented the most showed up. There's nobody in the bed now.

I wondered how they could forget. And I heard my mother tell them to get off of him. Heard him asking them, "Have you been a good boy? You going to school? You doing your schoolwork? Don't be like your daddy." I laid there and bit the covers, kicked the sheet, and said to myself, "Don't you worry, motherfucker. Don't you worry."

I was scared to death because I wanted to walk out there, but I wasn't. I wanted to throw my arms around him and hug him, kiss him.

Mom brought him in and she said, "Richard, your daddy's here." She said, "Oh Big Pres, he waited up all night for you. He knew you were coming. He bought you something for Christmas. You know he buys you something every Christmas. Richard!"

You know what it feels like to lay in bed and have your mother pull on you? You know you're not asleep, but you're not going to move. She rolls you over and there's a face full of tears. He said, "What's wrong, son?" Have her look at him, not to embarrass him because he's a stranger in his own house, and all strangers have to be treated with respect and hear her tell him, "Big Pres, he's just jealous. He's just jealous because you didn't pick him up like you picked up the rest of them."

"Didn't you hear me call for you, Richard? Did you hear me say, 'Daddy's home'? What are you crying about? Are you sick?"

As I laid there in that bed and looked up, he looked like he was ten feet tall. Clean, healthy. He sat down on the bed, and I heard Mama say, "Don't sit on that dirty bed." We had one sheet that stayed on the bed for six months.

He got up and brushed it off. She walked out and pulled out one of the silk linen tablecloths the white folks gave her, which we'd never be able to use, and covered up the bed so he could sit there and talk to me. She walked out and she kept the rest of the kids out of the room. Course she didn't have to keep them out. They were busy, looking at the money he gave them. Then he looked at me and said, "I brought you some money." I said, "I don't want it." He said, "I got more for you than I had for them." I said, "I still don't want it." He said, "Don't you want to see me? I'm your daddy, boy."

I said, "I see you every time I see that little woman in there on her knees on the floor, looking out the window, crying and praying that you'd come. You know, you ought to thank me because I brought you here tonight. Thank me that you never get sick because every night I say my prayers, I say, 'Bless him wherever he is.'"

He said, "I'm gonna stay home with y'all this time if y'all want me. Do you want me to stay, Richard? I'm going to get a job."

I looked at him, and I saw that look I'd always see on his face when he was telling the truth. When he felt ashamed and felt guilty. And wanted to get close to a family of his own. I didn't say anything to him. Said it to myself. "If he stays, I'll leave. I don't need you, old man. No, I don't need you. I needed you when the boys would chase me home. I needed you when Mr. Ben would curse me. I needed you when the man cheated me out of some money and knew he was cheating me. I needed you every time Boo's daddy came home at seven o'clock."

He looked at me and said, "Are you sick?" My mother walked in. He said, "'Cille, I think I'll take him to the doctor tomorrow." I kind of smiled because I didn't want to go to a doctor.

Then he got up, and he asked her, "'Cille, what's wrong with him?"

She said, "Don't worry about him. He's crazy."

Do you know what it feels like to have your mother stand over you and call you crazy? Do you know what it feels like to have a mother lose all the passionate love she had for you the day before, to pacify a dog? A dog that's not even worth being pacified?

Then he said what I knew he would say. "You got a drink, 'Cille?"

He didn't even have the decency to drink it out of a glass. Drank it right out of the bottle. And that's the day I knew you could say a prayer and get it answered, then end up hating yourself and cursing God.

* * *

Sure enough, that night he beat her. Do you know what it feels like when a man beats a woman all the way through her house, cursing her and kicking her, and knocking her down, and telling her about his women? And telling her she thinks she's so goddamn good that he doesn't even feel right walking down the street with you, because when I walk down the street, everybody wants to run up and say hello to you and look at me like I'm dirt.

"What have you taught Richard? Whatever you taught them, you can't turn all of them against me."

Do you know what it feels like to hear those same kids that were jumping up, hollering, screaming, yelling, and shouting, then praising and bragging over the money that he gave them? Do you know what it feels like to see your sister laying over in the bed crying, your brothers so goddamn scared they don't know what to do?

And I laid there and looked at him whip her. Looked at him knock her down. He was saying the things to her I wanted to warn her about that day when he walked in and she said I was crazy.

Then he walked over to the bed where I was laying, and he beat me too.

That was the mistake he made. After all, when he beat me, he beat the wrong one because he beat somebody that didn't love him.

Do you know what it feels like to hear a man come back thirty minutes later, crying and apologizing, telling her how much he loved her? And listening to her tell him it was her fault. That all she was trying to do was tell him that she wanted to get off relief.

I got up, went into the kitchen, and got the butcher knife. Didn't know how strong he was while he was sitting there with his head in his hands crying. I swung at him. In taverns I'd seen too many people swing with a knife not to know what I was doing. I swung at him for every kid in the world who hated their daddy.

Mom stopped me. Mom grabbed the knife. He looked up. Guess it's a hell of a thing for a daddy to look in his own son's eyes and see murder.

I think for the first time in his life, he realized what he'd done because I heard him telling Mama, "I'll leave. I'll leave now. And don't beat Richard. You should've let him hit me with it. I need to be dead. Never been no good, never treated them right."

I watched him turn and walk out the door. Listened to her hold the door while he was pulling it closed, then her pulling it until it slammed. And when it slammed, she fell all the way down the hall because the knob came off in her hand.

The kids stood at the window crying, "Don't leave, Daddy. Don't leave, Daddy!" I walked to the window and felt like I was daddy. I felt like I stood taller than anybody in the house. I stood and I looked at him walk.

Then I got up from the window and went out the back door to follow him. Man, if I live to get a thousand years old, I'll always thank God that I did. Followed him into a tavern. Came in behind him. Got there just in time to hear a woman arguing with him about where he had been, and hearing him say, "I couldn't get away."

In fifteen minutes' worth of time, all the shame was gone. He was going to leave anyway. I just gave him a reason, an excuse because he was running late. Heard him say, "I had to beat the bitch's ass for talking about you." He said, "But I got a little boy, little Richard. He's a motherfucker."

* * *

I wonder how many men have kids at home waiting on them, that want them to come home? Guess that's why I dig my little daughters.

I guess that's why my wife, Lil, gets so upset because she thinks I wanted to have a boy as most men do. She doesn't know every time a baby is born, I wanted one of mine to be a girl. Because I'd rather take the chance on raising another Lucille Gregory for the world than a Presley Gregory. The whole world would be better off if it had nothing but Lucilles and no Presleys at all.

Wonder if that clown knew what he missed when he'd come home and what he thought was fatherly love was excitement for a stranger. Every time I walk into my house, my little daughter walks up to me and she'll say, "I love you, Daddy." Yeah, he never heard that. Heard it from some woman in the street, but he never heard it from his kids. And every time I hear it from mine, I wonder if he only knew what he was missing.

"I love you, Daddy" means more than all the sevens falling on all the craps tables all over the world. I wonder if he knows what it feels like to hear one little kid tell her little sister, "Daddy's sick." That means more than all the doctors in the world when you can lay in one of them beds, pain and misery, sick and tired, and hear a little kid say, "Daddy's sick." Wonder if he knows what it feels like to be able to put his arms around his kids and squeeze them so tight sometimes you forget how hard you're squeezing them because you're enjoying it.

I wonder if he knows what he missed.

I wonder about him, laying out there in San Francisco, a good man now that can sit back and boast about his kids.

I wonder what happens to this man every time he picks up a paper and he reads about Dick Gregory. I wonder if he's still foolish enough to believe that his leaving helped us. Because I'd turn in all the Dick Gregorys in the world, and all the nightclub performances I've ever had, and all the big money I've ever made, to go back through those days with a daddy.

But I learned something from him. Learned how to respect a mother.

It's a horrible thing for a mother to have to come home and look in the pot and see the food is running out, going to bed every night with poverty, going to bed every night with the bills.

Kids don't want to hear all about where you been, where you're coming from, how high coffee is, who got drunk last night, who they caught embezzling something. All they want you to do is be a daddy.

The sweetest feeling in the world is to be able to come home after the whole world done kicked you in your ass and be able to walk through that house and walk to that baby's bed, see those kids laying there safe and sound. With the expression on their face like Mama's in bed and Daddy's coming.

It's a wonderful feeling to see them grow up. I even notice my kids' ears growing, and that's something men don't do that aren't with them twenty-four hours a day. See their feet get big.

See them understand things. See them curious about things.

Your kid is the only kid in the world that you can walk in and give him $500 in $1 bills, and they'll play with it till they get tired. They'll leave it on the floor and they'll get in your lap.

It's a wonderful feeling to be able to come home one day and have your kids crawl into bed with you, lay down and go to sleep just because Daddy's asleep. And to lay there and peep at them. Feel them put their little hands around you and hug you. See them steal a kiss when they think you're asleep. Feel those little delicate, warm hands playing with your beard.

The greatest feeling in the world is to feel a kid's hand on your nose. Funny thing, my babies will never grab anybody's nose but their daddy's and their mama's. They'll never put their hand in anybody's mouth but daddy's mouth or mommy's mouth. Any man that has a kid that doesn't want to run in and stick a hand in his mouth, and he tries to bite her finger, he's not a daddy. Because as dangerous as she knows it is, she still knows you're not going to hurt her. The greatest feeling in the world is to have your kid walk up to you and ask you to do something they would ask no other man to do. "Pick me up and throw me in the air!" And look at them get frightened when they go up and laugh like hell when they come down, and you catch them. The greatest thing in the world.

And I wonder now about my daddy. He hasn't got the right to pick mine up because he cheated. Didn't pick up his own.

You don't qualify to give my kids a birthday or Christmas present because he didn't give his one. My kids will always honor him as a grandpa. They'll never hear nothing but nice things about him as far as being a granddaddy, but he couldn't reach and beat me with his belt, it's that same gap. He can't reach and throw his grandkids up in the air.

Wonder what it felt like for a man that roamed the streets around the country, and every time he saw a kid, he had to stop and wonder what his were doing. Or was he just that dirty that he just gave us up and thought we were in jail somewhere?

He had nerve enough to tell me I was going to be like him when I grow up.

If I thought this minute I would have a boy that would grow up and be like him to another woman or their kids, I would pray to all the gods in all the heavens to destroy me now. Destroy me now with the most pain you could ever destroy a man with.

I guess where you have a good mother and no father, God kind of sits in. It's not good enough, but it helps. I got kind of tired of hearing Mama say, "God, fix it so I could pay the rent. God, fix it so the lights could be turned on." As much as I honored that and respected that, I kind of felt like that wasn't his job. Plus, a kid kind of likes to see who's doing those things so you can tell them thanks.

But he walked away and left us. Left us to face the cold winters, the hot summers. The Easters with nothing new. The picnics with nothing in the basket. And I wonder if it ever dawned on him that he had it so there was one Sunday we couldn't even go to church: Father's Day.

When I swung at him with that knife, had I known then what I know now, I probably would have fell on my knees and cried for him.

No kid in the world should ever raise a hand to swing at a no-good daddy. No woman in the world should ever lose sleep for hating a no-good father. Because that's already been taken care of in that beautiful parable, "A man who destroys his own home shall inherit the wind."

DEVELOPING HIS GIFTS

CULTURAL OPPORTUNITIES IN ST. LOUIS

The school system [in St. Louis] was very good because the St. Louis Symphony Orchestra would do concerts for the schoolkids. We'd get half a day from school to go downtown. It was a wonderful feeling sitting there, seeing the people with the violins and the conductor, sophisticated with the tux on and everything.

Probably one of the greatest assets a kid had in St. Louis, as far as culture was concerned, was the Muny Opera. Bob Hope came in and played in the original *Roberta*. I was able to see *Show Boat*, all of the top operas, all of your top Broadway plays, when I was a little hoodlum back home. We used to say we were the only hoodlums with culture! You could snatch a pocketbook in St. Louis and be whistling a tune from *Carousel* while doing it. We got to see all the top operas from June to September, and we'd go every night because they had free seats. There was something about this type of music that I would come home, and I would just feel like I was somebody. It was a wonderful feeling to be able to turn on the radio, the stuff that you never listened to, and to be able to turn it on and can hum it or whistle the whole opera all the way through.

It was miles from our house, but we'd take off at six o'clock and get to the opera just about the time it was starting. We would go in, rent the opera glasses (15 cents to rent the glasses, $2 deposit). I used to live for the day when I could go out with my $2 in my pocket.

You never missed it on Sunday night. Gang wars wouldn't start till after the opera was over. It was a wonderful, beautiful affair. It was outdoors. You'd just sit way up, so far you couldn't tell if the performers were white or Black. It was a good feeling during intermission to be able to walk down and walk in between the rich people that were out there, down on the front-row seats. It was a beautiful thing to be able to do this.

What I liked best about it . . . this was the only time that I could identify with the rich man because I knew he was sitting down front, and he was seeing the same thing I was seeing.

I don't know what would have happened to this country had the richest man and the poorest man not been able to seek some form of entertainment after a day's or week's work. In the neighborhood we lived in, we would go to the place where you paid 15 cents for a bottle of beer and you caught a honky-tonk show. That entertainment was just as important as the guy spending $100 for a table because you had a place where you could go and leave yourself to sit and look at a performer. Every city in America should have free sections where they can get top performers because it's a hell of a thing for a kid to be able to identify with top show business people, people that you idolize, people that you read about every day.

TRACK AND FIELD

At night I would lay down in bed and I couldn't sleep for wanting tomorrow to get there, so I could get out on the track, so tomorrow would be over, so Saturday we could have our track meet.

This was a whole new period in my life. Nothing was interesting to me anymore. It was all track and rightfully so because I was never anybody until I had track. To get the feeling that I got out of track . . . that's a clean, beautiful, honest-to-goodness feeling. You are participating in a sport where there's no monetary reward; there's no professional guarantee. You're out there all by yourself. You can't blame it on anybody. You can't get out there and have a guy dislike you because one guy is getting all the glory. Track's not like that.

Track was so beautiful for my mind. I caught myself praying one day and I had to stop because it dawned on me. What right do I have asking you to help me win? How disrespectful can I be to the other? Because when I ask for you to help me win, I've completely canceled out the others. Actually, I'm praying for their loss. So then I quit praying.

When I came to the line, I realized and I prayed different. Going to bed every night and training right, trying to keep rules, the laws, the regulations, if I can't win the race with this, may the best man win. But I had the attitude that I'm bringing to the line 118 pounds of bones. I'm bringing to the line a body that was frail and had missed many good meals, a body that has been well kept in the last year, that has laid down the law for training. Now, if you can bring something better than this . . . I take my hat off to you. It's absolutely your race.

This was the attitude I formed on running. You find out things when you're out there. It's a hell of a thing, and I think it'd be a better world today if every man the world over could extend himself to complete exhaustion. Complete exhaustion for good at the end.

I've had track meets that got so damn hot in St. Louis . . . 110, 109. In the wintertime in cross-country, your hands get so cold; your feet get so cold. I've had track meets that I swore, after this race is over, as God is my witness, I'll never run track again. This is how grinding those races would get.

It's an individual sport. You're out there all by yourself. Nobody can help you. I used to get real nervous the night before a race. I used to lay up in bed and think about all the boys that had a chance of winning. I'd get up the next morning, and I'd be so damn tired I couldn't move. I found out beyond a shadow of a doubt that a man loses just as much energy, physically and mentally, laying up in bed the night before a race as you do out there on that track. You re-enact the whole race. You close your eyes. You see him coming. You go that whole mile. You can imagine how tired I am now mentally. I lost a race because of that. So now I decided that I would never, as long as I live, worry.

I knew that if I didn't break this habit in high school, I was going to take it into college. And you get to the point where you are so used to worrying over a meet that I used to worry on Saturdays when we didn't even have track meets. I was so used to worrying, at nighttime when everybody was going to a party, I would go out to Public School Stadium and just get on the track.

It was the only thing I had where I was somebody. It was the only thing that I ever touched that made me. So, anytime I needed anything, I used to just go out and lay out on the track and on the grass, and just thank the gods in heaven because I couldn't believe this thing here. I used to go out and just look at the empty stands, and then laugh about how full they were during a track meet, and made myself believe I brought 'em in.

Track was a background to all of the things that have happened to me.

It was the attention-getter that I needed. It was the discipline that I needed.

I had too much inside of me for it not to be channeled some way where I could do it all by myself. On a team, nothing. It had to be track. I'd get aggravated about a situation, and just go and run. I would get up at five o'clock in the morning and run around the square block in front of my house. I was not running to be in shape. I was running so the working people that'd be going to work that early would see and know me. I would get up every morning. I would run around that block from five-thirty to eight o'clock. Constantly, constantly. For attention.

When you run and get mentally and physically tired together, you're a different man. When I would run around the block, I could concentrate. I could think. And nine times out of ten, whenever I wanted to think, I would run.

I wasn't training. I was out there running, trying to get something off my mind. I was out there running because something happened that I didn't understand, that I was trying to figure out. So I ran. And I ran. And I ran.

I go into my last year, there are many things that are happening to me. Many things racially that people slammed me in the face with. But these things were minor because I had that one stick. I had the old neutralizer. I'm not inferior to anyone. Okay, your daddy's a good chemist; I'm a good miler. Your daddy lives up there on the hill? Well, goddamn it, if he ever comes down on the track, you're in my kingdom. And when I come up there, I'll be in yours, but I might practice and take yours away from you one day. Because I found out through track that if you practice, you put in the time and the effort and the sacrifice, and build up to what you want, then you can move up to that block, and say, "Okay, baby, I'm in the race now."

SUMNER HIGH SCHOOL BAND

I had to get an eight o'clock class, so I went in to the band director. We had one of the best high school bands in the world, bar none. I asked him, "Could I get in the band?" He asked had I had any music, who I had studied under, and could I read music. I told him I'd never been in nothing, and he told me this was the senior band, everybody in there had music for at least ten years. So I explained to him that I had to get an early class because I was working in the steel mill, got off at seven and I could get there at eight. And I'd get out of school at two. I could practice track and go home and sleep. He told me I could if I came in early and cleaned up the band room and had all the music put out. So I signed up for senior band and I got in it.

In the process of being in the senior band, I used to steal the music and take it home at night and take it to work with me. Eventually I learned how to play it. I still can't read music, but the drummer who played timpani drums was sick one day, and we were getting ready for a big concert. The band director was real shook up, and I got on those drums one day, and the guy never got his job back. As a matter of fact, I had some scholarships in music when I finished high school.

This was a very important part of my life in high school, because we made long trips and had band concerts. We played very heavy music: Beethoven, Bach, Mozart, anybody you could name. He prided himself on being able to play the hardest music. We would study six months, night and day, just to get ready for one concert, and then go to one state final. I never will forget the day that we had our big concert. It's my first big break as far as music was concerned.

Long as I live, I'll always remember that he knew I couldn't play music, and he had that whole band to direct. But yet and still, there was some kind of way he would look at me and let me know I'm not supposed to be playing. He would always nod his head when it came time for me to come in. He did this three solid years without missing it. And eventually when I went away to college, I joined the college symphony band. This guy did the same thing. It's just unbelievable the communication system they have. Then I played in the marching band, and this was probably the biggest thrill, to march in a parade. I think this was the thing that topped it all off, the parades that you marched in. I played bass drum, which is the most important thing in the marching band.

Then all the football games. It was a great thrill because in the wintertime during football season, I ran cross-country. And during halftime, I came right in from cross-country and played music in the band. When I went to college, I did the same thing. A lot of cross-country meets they'd start before the halftime. We'd run around and go outside the football stadium and come back in, and I had a lot of good times and won a lot of races because I was in a hurry to get back so I could get my bass drum and play in the band.

This was the period when my mother came to the first concert and sat up in the balcony. She wasn't sitting down front with the rest of the mothers. I looked up in the balcony and there she sat. I didn't know who I resented the most, Mom or the system there. She was so happy while she was sitting there. No mother in the whole place could light it up like my mother, because she just couldn't conceive . . . she just couldn't believe what she was hearing.

NAVIGATING A WIDER WORLD

ACCIDENTAL ACTIVIST

Before school started back, I waited for that [high school record] book to come out. I didn't see my name listed in the *Scholastic Yearbook*, so I went downtown. Hickey, who was the superintendent of schools, was not in. I talked to someone in his office and asked him why I was not listed in the book. They explained to me that you run up in Jefferson City at the all-Negro track meet—and it's just as good as ours—but for some reason or another, they don't list the Negro track meet.

But he was sure that *Pittsburgh Courier* carried it. That's when I decided that I was going to be listed, and I was going to get credit. I went back home, I talked to my coach, and I asked him why wasn't I listed. He told me I had to run with the white boys before I get listed. This coach of mine was Warren St. James, who had gone to Southern Illinois University and ran the distance runs and taught me an awful lot about distance. Taught me how to win.

I decided to talk to a group that was organizing a march on the Board of Education about overcrowded conditions. We'd planned to walk out of school when we started back that September. There was a lot of tension in the school. I didn't feel right walking out.

Seemed like everybody that had decided to walk out were always getting put out of school or getting in trouble. And still, I knew the grown people involved were ethical and moral.

When we walked out that school door, it seemed like many people were afraid. Pop Beckett [a physical education teacher and mentor] ran up to me with a baseball bat. He said, "Gregory, don't walk out that door." I said, "Pop, I have to. I have to for myself, and I have to for Mama. Mama didn't know I was one of the best milers in the country this year. Mama's gonna find out." I joined them at the last minute. We marched out, and the kids from other schools marched out too.

We marched downtown, and in getting downtown, by moving from one end of the line to the other, the press thought that I was the leader. They came and talked to me about it, asked me what we're marching for. I told them we were marching because of over-crowded conditions, and I was marching because my name didn't show up in the scholastic book, and I wanted my mother to know. We met and marched to City Hall. The job that I had was running from the front end of the line to the back end, telling people to stay in line, watch the traffic. Don't do anything that's gonna give us a bad name.

Nobody could understand what this was. It was like it turned the town upside down.

We stood there, and the people at City Hall came out and listened to the leaders. When I got back to school, everybody was telling me I was going to be expelled. They said some people thought it was communist-inspired. My mother asked me about it: "Was it communists that had anything to do with it?" I said, "Mom, I don't even know how to spell *communism*."

Then the next week, the district integrated the track program and the cross-country program. This is when things really start to open.

SOUTHERN ILLINOIS UNIVERSITY

Warren St. James was short, very collegiate, very sensitive, and very touchy. He was the type of coach who worked hard when he was running in college, but he was never the winner. I think everything where he fell short in track he wanted for me.

This is when I really started to develop. This is when I found out about pushing that extra mile when you didn't have to in training, and found out that this is the thing that gave you the edge. He was with me all the time. He was like my father. He would come by in the morning, he would always come and check the class where I was. And then he was the one that suggested I go to Southern Illinois University. I decided to go. When I went to college, I needed someone's concern, someone who had been there and knew certain things about it so I didn't go in completely blank on it. He came through at the right time. Had it not been for Warren and track, I would have gone far enough just to find another disappointment.

I knew nothing about training for distance. There weren't too many Black coaches in St. Louis that knew that much about training for the long-distance races. We had predominantly controlled the short dashes. Warren was probably one of the most excellent coaches in the country as far as distance running is concerned, and he gave me free what he bought and paid for.

I arrived at Southern Illinois University in March of '52 (we were on the quarter system there). I got there on a Greyhound bus with my shopping bag—Mom had put some food in there, which embarrassed me a whole lot. I never will forget that day I arrived on campus. It's wonderful to be the greatest thing in your community, which is the world when this is all you know. You go in with respect for your past record, but the attitude there on campus meant I had to do a complete physical breakdown of this starship and start all over again to prove it there. When I arrived at Southern Illinois University, the pride in being able to look back over what I came through, and the things I had been through, and say, "You made it! You're here."

Just the thought of being in college fascinated me so much nothing else mattered. It was like I had defied the whole system to get there. I never will forget entering the first day, seeing the kids on the campus, getting to meet new faces, getting to meet people that hadn't heard of me, and then just enough people dealing with athletics that did know of you. The bulk of students were from small towns that had never heard of Dick Gregory. And this was a thrill to be able to come out and give me a chance to get to know them from the ground. Not because I came from St. Louis as a big athlete, but to prove myself there.

This was the first time I had been thrown in with this many white folks. This was the first time I had a white instructor. This is where the integration of high school track helped me tremendously: talking to the white kids who I ran against, meeting the white coaches, and then having the respect of whites simply through running track. There were many things that happened in college that I don't know how I would have adjusted to, just coming out of the old, segregated neighborhood, all segregated school, and being thrown in there where the most kids we had (out of four thousand) was four hundred Black. It showed because the Blacks were always together. The Blacks that didn't run in bunches were the ones coming from communities with integrated schools and integrated neighborhoods.

But there in Carbondale, Illinois, every chance we had, we would go downtown to the Black section and hang out. The same way we did when we were in St. Louis.

The whites thought it was a rare privilege when they were invited to go with you. This was like a myth to them, like many things in this country are myths to whites. Although they were accepted in our neighborhood, many people feel that the Black community is segregated. The Blacks are segregated *against*, but we do not segregate. Many places we would go to in Carbondale, whites just assumed they weren't accepted, mainly because we were not accepted in many of the white places in town.

"OUTSTANDING ATHLETE OF THE YEAR"

I developed my personality, tried to get me an attitude. Talking to the teachers, talking to the kids, I tried to find out why is it I'm twenty years old and I've never seen this many white folks in my life. And I *knew* they got more white folks in St. Louis than at Southern Illinois University. I used to see them in parades, see them on Election Day. White folks come out and give us a picnic on Election Day. Pick up little Black babies peeing all over them, patting them on the back, give them some ice cream. Never did see those old white folks no more until the next election. Matter of fact, couldn't even go back to that park no more until the next election.

So I'm fascinated, trying to find out what makes white folks tick. Figured I got to get this white piece of paper from SIU. Get on out there with them. It's a white man's world I'm living in, so maybe I'm supposed to have to learn how to act white. Damn, I don't want to learn how to act white, though. I look around and one of them is committing suicide, another is selling a secret to another country. I got to wonder, do I want to be like this man? Sometimes when you sit back and look at it, figure out what's happening, it's probably the world's greatest comedy. Just sit back and laugh yourself to death. That's what it was coming to.

I started getting hung up in social life in college, and trying to learn white folks, trying to get me a white piece of paper, to go out and get me one of those white folks' jobs. Then I'd see so many Black kids graduating from that white school end up in the post office, end up delivering mail, end up driving cabs. Here I'm living in a white man's world, going to his school, fixing to get a piece of paper, and damn near forgot he's going to send me out there with that Black face.

So if I sat there for four years, and read all the books, and not gotten me an attitude, I would have walked out Phi Beta Kappa, straight As on my transcript, not knowing that when I walked into the big department store, before I could even tell them I made all As in accounting, they'd tell me they're not hiring porters today. We don't need no elevator operators today.

Maybe that's why so many of our top Blacks are so upset. They're fighting a double thing. It's the worst thing in the world to be a soldier, and they don't put no ammunition in your gun. They gave us a bad school to go to when we were kids, and when I decide to go to that white school, they want to give me the same test they give that white boy. They even give a horse a handicap. Then again, maybe they're right, maybe he can look and see he's made me so strong, he better put some weight on my back. Give the handicap to that other boy because I think he needs it.

So I'm in college, having a ball too. Running all the track in the world, got a wonderful coach. Doc Lingle was his name. Hell of a man. One of the few men in the country I've ever met who can take an athlete and make a man out of him first. Made such a hell of a man out of me I never lost no races no more. Finished second a couple times, but I didn't lose them—another man won it.

As I developed, I was very confused, because I was seeing things going on. Every time I go past the athletic department, I don't see anything but Black athletes' pictures hanging up, until I looked at the top of the ceiling at "Outstanding Athletes of the Year." Not one Black had ever won, so I decided to get my name up there. I came down here to try and get me attitude and ended up in a struggle. Not a Black struggle. No, I've always been an individual first, an American second, and a Black third. I qualify to be up there. Let me get out and see what I can do, talk to the people. I got me an attitude now. I found out how they were doing it. I just walked over and told my coach if I don't make outstanding athlete of the year, I'm going to quit.

So I'm sitting there that night, and everybody's nervous, wondering who they're gonna pick. They even flew one of the big sports commentators down from St. Louis for the big awards. They called my name. "Dick Gregory, Outstanding Athlete of the Year."

I felt kind of bad I had to get that honor with a threat, although I did deserve it. I sat there nervous and scared. But I was so cool that they couldn't even hate me enough to give it to another Black because I didn't go in as a Black, I went in as an individual, and made them think it wasn't anything pertaining to race.

Somebody had to break the system. I couldn't do anything but run track. Never picked up a basketball, couldn't play baseball, didn't know how to swim yet. They gave it to me, though. This broke the ice. Then they gave it to another black person, and we've been making it ever since.

The sports commentator went back to St. Louis, did a thirty-minute show, talking about Dick Gregory, greatest athlete ever to hit Southern Illinois University. St. Louis boy!

Yep, I ran a lot of track, got to know a lot about life and white folks.

Even got in the Theta Xi Variety Show. I was doing satire and didn't even know what satire was. I won the variety show, and the fraternity I was in thought we all should have won, but we didn't raise no hell because they didn't want to give everything to Blacks that night. We didn't complain. We went out and bought a little trophy though because we knew we won it.

It was the first time I ever got up in front of a crowd of white folks and talked. Made them laugh. I kind of thought, "Man, this is almost as good a feeling as winning a track meet." But I'm a little safer running track, because it's much easier running against a white boy than trying to get one of them to laugh at you, because he might be mad at you. Everything you're saying might be funny as hell and he might not laugh. But there ain't nothing he can do with his feelings on that track.

I had a different thing going there. In high school, I was just fighting being poor and being on relief. In college, I was fighting being Black for the first time in my life. When I was fighting just being poor in St. Louis and ran one of them good track meets on Saturday, it made me the hero until the next Saturday rolled around. Then I went out on the track and recharged my battery again.

It was a hell of a thing down there at SIU, running well. All the manhood I used to get out of running on that track, they used to steal from me every time I walked off of it.

VARSITY THEATER

With the last penny I had, I went to the movie in Carbondale with a friend of mine, Leo Wilson, a Black man. Walked in and Leo broke for the balcony. I see the white usher standing there and I said, "I'll take care of you next time. I haven't got no money."

He smiled and said, "Okay, aren't you Dick Gregory?"

I said, "Yeah."

He said, "We've heard a lot about you. It's nice to have you here at Southern Illinois University."

I said, "Thanks a lot." Then I run on up with Leo.

It was the coolest place I'd been in since I arrived. Wasn't nothing in the balcony but Blacks. There were a bunch of athletes, so I felt like we had the balcony made. Looked around and saw a couple of white folks up there. I started going to the movies, and sometimes I'd tip the guy and go up in the balcony, it felt so good sitting up there.

Then one day, I promised one girl I was going to take her to the movies, and decided to take another girl, and walked into that movie and sat downstairs.

I didn't even know what was happening. Didn't even know the movie theater was segregated. All I remembered was when I was a kid, you lived for the day you could sit upstairs in the balcony, not realizing it was an all-Black movie theater. So you'd pay top dollar to sit in the balcony.

I didn't realize I'd been tipping that white boy for nothing. Didn't realize he was telling me it was a pleasure having me in this town while I'm on my way up to the segregated section. Never realized that when the balcony got full, and there were plenty of seats downstairs, you had to stand. Didn't even realize when the girl jerked back and said, "I don't want to sit down here." I'm so busy thinking I don't want to run across that other girl, I said, "Come on, baby, you're with me."

Sat down and noticed people looking at me, but I thought they were looking at Dick Gregory the athlete. Then the usher walks down and says, "Greg, I'm sorry, but you have to go upstairs."

I said, "That's okay. I'll sit down here tonight. Everything will be all right." I started to ask him to lean down so I could tell him why I couldn't go up in the balcony, about the girl I was supposed to have up there, and how I didn't want her to see me.

Then his attitude changed. "I said you have to go upstairs." I thought he was playing. Then I figured maybe he wanted the tip that I usually give him. So now a commotion is going on. Everybody's looking at me, and he said, "I'll be back."

He comes back with the manager, who says, "Mr. Gregory, can I see you?" That's when I knew something was wrong. When white folks call you "Mister," something's wrong. I told the girl, "I'll be right back." Never knew I was leaving her down there with all that hell. The Blacks upstairs in the balcony started saying, "My man!" "Go, baby, go!" They were cheering me. I thought it was because of last Saturday's victory.

I walked upstairs, and the manager breaks it to me. "You can't sit downstairs." I asked why. "The Black seats are in the balcony here. It's the only place you can sit." Man, I was destroyed. He'd ruined my whole myth. All I wanted was the day I could get myself into a position where I can always sit in the balcony. Now he tells me that that's my place?

I'm so confused because I didn't know if the guy back home in the Black theater had been cheating me for all those years, or this guy here was trying to destroy something I had.

So I told him to put me up there, and he called the police. When the cop walked up, I couldn't help but realize how many times I had slipped by the theater in St. Louis, laid $2 on the usher to save me a balcony seat, and when I got there, the usher had gone and the balcony was full. I thought about how many times I wanted to call the police and either get my $2 back or get the policeman to make them put me up in the balcony.

Now here's a man calling the police to make me get up in the balcony.

I was so disgusted and so horrified. I had to go get the young lady because I realized what I'd left her down there with. I went and I got her, and I left with my head well tucked. As I walked out the door, the last thing the guy said was, "Be sure and get your money back."

I paid to see a movie, and I ended up going through the heaviest drama. No man alive could have written a script for what went on that night. If they had to pay me for what I went through, all the money in the world wouldn't have paid it. So I looked back at him and said, "Keep it. I'll be back."

The next night I went back by myself, and I sat downstairs. They said I was crazy. They gave me the okay: "Let him sit downstairs, he's crazy." So I brought some other people with me that might not be crazy, that might not be doing it because they're Dick Gregory, the athlete at Southern Illinois University. Had I thought about it, I should have asked my coach or asked the president of the university. Or asked the mayor, who taught there.

In 1953, Hollywood produced the movie *The Robe*. This little theater in Carbondale paid a lot of money to get that movie. We sat downstairs one day, and the manager asked me to come up to his office. He was scared to death.

Economics won out. He told me about the money he'd paid for this movie, and he asked me not to sit there while the movie was on because he didn't want to lose customers. But right after the movie, it would be okay.

I'm so damn sick and tired of negotiating for my rights, I don't know what to do. Force against persuasion, I guess. So I said okay, and after that, every time I'd go I'd sit downstairs. And I hated it because up in the balcony is where I really wanted to go, but I couldn't.

Everybody will tell you there that knew me, he's happy-go-lucky; he was jolly. But I was dying a slow death.

CARBONDALE

It's a hell of a thing when you're a grown man and you walk down the street and look at your buddies on the track team with you, and all you can do is look through the window.

Never will forget one guy. I looked at him sitting in a restaurant eating a steak sandwich with his girl. And as I looked through the window and saw all of the athletes' pictures hanging up around the wall, I didn't see mine. And damn glad because it would be a hell of a thing to know my picture could get in, while I couldn't. I waved at the guy and said to myself, "I'll crush him tomorrow on the track."

If I went back and checked the books, I'd guess the Black flunk-out rate was pretty high. That school kept us so separated we had to have two dances on homecoming. One with the white folks, and then we went in town and had our own that night. Had a ball too. No Blacks were on the student council, so Sauter-Finegan came in with his muted tuba and the hottest tune he played was "Don't Waltz Around the Mulberry Bush with Anyone Else but Me." You kept me downtown next to that funky Black tavern, and all I heard was that gutbucket blues, so that's all I wanted to hear at my college homecoming. I was kind of proud I could go too because I could get even with the white folks for the [segregated] restaurants I had to walk past.

"Where you going, Greg?"

"I got a little party to go to. See you tomorrow!"

I imagine it would have been fun to sit around with the boys on the track team after the season was over and drink beer. Couldn't take them out to my side of town because they just had one Black cop there. His only beat was patrolling the two Black taverns, and he owned one of them. Didn't want them to see that.

This was the town of Carbondale. That's where I first learned the bitterness of racial prejudice. That's when I first realized how deep it was. With all that misery and pain, I bit my lip and grinned, and stuck with it long enough to weed out some good white folks. Old guy at the clothing store, I could sit there and talk with him. Used to go out and buy stuff I didn't even need, just to be able to walk in that section of town and go in some place. Old guy who had the cleaners there, he really made me feel good. I could get credit there.

I sat back to look at the people on campus. The president was a beautiful guy, Dr. Morris. Hell of a man. Made a hell of a school out of that place. I sit back now and wonder why he didn't break down all the segregation laws. Wonder why he didn't check on the prejudiced teachers. Had one teacher down there, when he wrote "Black" on the board, he put it in a small n. I waited until class was out, came back, and made the N the length of the blackboard.

It's a funny thing to sit in the stands and hear a guy sitting right behind you say, "Look at that nigger go!" And then a white boy would dive at him, and that Black brother would shake loose and keep going, and you want to look back at that man and say, "Call him another nigger!"

Any team that came to Southern Illinois University and had more Blacks than ours did, that's the one the Blacks secretly pulled for. People used to wonder, and I even had the dean ask me one time, "How come the Blacks sit by themselves? You're all free here." Because we don't want y'all to see us pulling for the other team that has the most Blacks on it. Yep, sit there during an [intrasquad] scrimmage and listen to the Blacks on your team come back and say how hard they hit a white boy, and you say, "Well, you should have broken his leg." Your own team. Then again, I guess the loyalty that the Black athletes have will always stick out. Whenever it was homecoming, we could have played against an all-Black team, and we wanted Southern Illinois to win. It's a hell of a feeling to sit there, and every time you see a Black on each side of the field get the ball, you hope he goes for a touchdown. And you still don't want your team to lose.

IN THE ARMY

I got drafted in the army. Went against the system the whole way because I didn't care. Didn't care about nothing. Didn't care about winning or losing, or living or dying.

I had fun while I was in the army. The army probably played a very important part in developing my show business career because I was so numb for those next three years that people in the army thought I was crazy. The things I'd say . . . An old colonel told me one time, "You must be a comedian. You go down to the social service club tonight and get on that show. If you don't win it, I'm going to court-martial you." I went down, and I won it. Not because I was worried about being court-martialed, but because I was funny. And I kept winning, and I kept winning, and I kept winning, and the next thing I knew, I was on an army tour and had qualified to go to the All-Army Show.

The winners from there go to *The Ed Sullivan Show*, and I prayed that night before I went to Fort Dix for that show. I said, "Lord, it is my wish that I win, but if it's not thy will, please let it not be done." Thank God I prayed that way, because had I won that show, I would have been destroyed as an entertainer. I would have gone to *The Ed Sullivan Show* in 1955 knowing nothing about show business, just being on the air as an accident. I would have thought I was a hell of an entertainer, and I would've had a different attitude. I toured all over with army shows. Never prepared anything, just got up and started talking. Social talk. System of the army. Didn't get court-martialed while I was there, never did anything bad, but I guess wearing blue suede shoes with your army uniform wasn't good. Or saluting with your left hand. Or calling a colonel a sergeant. Or going on KP and asking to be paid.

I never will forget that funny feeling when I got out of the army. The day before you get out, they ask you about your address. For the first time in my life, I realized I didn't have a home. Mama's gone. It's a helluva feeling when you have to give the government your address, and you have to give them Southern Illinois University, Carbondale, Illinois. That's where I live.

I WAS TRYING TO BE KING

Now, the training started.

Three nights a week, I had to get out in the street and find strange people and talk to them and try to develop material.

I used to hang out at a Walgreens drugstore and catch the people coming down for their lunch hour to develop material on.

Friends helped me get some clothes on credit. Used them as a reference to say I had been in Chicago a long time. The guy I was working for at the Esquire Lounge let me jack up my price and say I was making $100 a week and had been there for four years. I guess when I went downtown to Lytton's department store, I convinced them. So I didn't feel too bad at work. I was a little funnier, and I was clean. I had new shoes, a new suit, a new shirt.

Keeping my clothes clean almost cost me more than I was making. I changed suits every show, changed shirts every show. Never had done that before in my life, but I had such tremendous respect for those people sitting out there. And for the first time in my life, I was able to get a feeling that I didn't have to beat another man in a track meet to get. I didn't have to feel like I was somebody at the expense of another man losing.

I remembered then what my mother told me a long time ago when I made a sly remark to her and said, "I wonder whose mother's son I'm going to beat this week."

She looked at me and said, "I wonder how those other mothers feel. I hope they're not as ashamed of their sons as I am proud of you. Then again, Richard, I guess they couldn't be, because I'd be just as proud of you at the thought that you got in the race as I am with you winning."

Now, for the first time in my life, I have something that's all mine. And I'm growing every day. I have people saying, "That's Dick Gregory," and man, I'm not coming off at nobody else's expense.

Things start opening up for me. For the first time since high school, I felt that thirsty taste again. I'm learning and I'm learning. I'm buying comedy records. A lot of guys accused me of stealing their material after I made it. Had I not bought anything but comedy records, I'd have felt like I was stealing their material. But I was so enthused over what I was doing that I trained for comedy the same way I trained for track. That's why they can accuse me till the day they die and I'll never feel ashamed, because I dug into the library and walked downtown and spent money for books I couldn't even afford. Old books, the same jokes they had on their records, I found them in those books. So I knew it wasn't theirs.

I'd get up on the stage and everybody would tell me, "You remind me of Redd Foxx, you remind me of Nipsey Russell, you remind me of Slappy White." Not because I was doing their material, but because these were the only Black comics that had made it. Every now and then somebody would say, "You remind me of Bob Hope. You remind me of Milton Berle," because of the topical stuff I was doing.

Every night my job was to watch television. I watched television from the time it came on in the morning until it went off at night. I had to learn entertainment.

I brought the same amount of dignity and honor and respect to show business that I carried to the track. When a man would walk into a nightclub and want to pay me to introduce him, to introduce his party, I never took his money. When people would throw money up on the stage, I never bent over to pick it up. There were some nights I had more money thrown up on the stage at me than I was getting for my three nights' work, but I would never let a man know I wasn't making $100 a night.

I dressed like I was making $100 a night. I walked like I was making $100 a night, and I talked like I was making $100 a night.

I was not a gladiator. I was trying to be king.

I wanted the same respect from the people out there that I was giving them.

I made it a policy that I would never go to a man's table if I thought the woman he was with in any shape, form, or fashion was giving me the eye. You can't give a man no more respect than that. And many times, there were some beautiful women sitting there, but I always took the attitude that this man is paying my salary—not much of a salary, but he doesn't know how much I'm making—and I have to give him this respect.

Between working three days a week, watching television (the Paar show, all the comedy shows, Ed Sullivan, every form of entertainment I could watch), then getting out in the daytime and catching the people and developing new material on them, and buying all the comedy books I could buy, yep, I was really proud of myself.

I was working too hard to really be concerned about anything but trying to develop. Trying to find out why a man is such a different animal when he's out enjoying himself. I guess it's the system. The system had whipped him down so hard. Why is it when a comic's up working, or an entertainer's up working, if they are very bad, the people pull for them to be good? And the least little funny thing you say, they'll laugh. That's why an entertainer has a hell of a debt he owes to that audience. That's why I go out of my way to do benefits, and go out of my way to try to help people, because every time I do a benefit, every time I help someone, I feel like I'm saying thanks to those ordinary people that pushed me all the way up to the top.

LIL

One Sunday, I looked in the audience and a girl walked up to me and said, "Would you come back to the table and give me your autograph? I'd like you to meet my sisters." I said yes. That's why it's always so nice to be polite to people. Be nice. Never put yourself above that audience. Because, in walking to that table, I didn't know I was going to meet my wife.

I walked over and there was a little girl sitting there, very bashful and very excited, like God had walked over to the table. I asked them where they were from. Willard, Ohio. A small town. This was the first time they had ever been out to see big entertainment. We were big to people who had never been in a nightclub before.

I sat down and asked her name. She said, "Lillian Smith." I asked her where she lived, and she told me. And during the conversation she told me she worked at the University of Chicago. I said, "Well, I'm over there every day running track. Let's have lunch one day." She said, "Oh, no, you don't mean it," and she kinda tucked her head like I was the big entertainer just saying something to be saying it. I said, "I'll tell you what. You give me your phone number and I'll call you and I'll let you know exactly what day." She was so nervous she could hardly write it.

I rolled this little piece of paper up and put it in my pocket. This was an afternoon show on Sunday. And when I went up to do the next show, I couldn't believe how she looked at me. Like she was afraid that nobody in Willard, Ohio, would ever believe that she talked to this man. I thought, it's going to give me a great thrill to call her 'cause she doesn't believe I'm going to call.

This was the summer of '58. They had stayed for the first (matinee), second, and third show. When I was ready to leave, I walked past the table and told them good night. I left with the girl I was dating at the time. I took her home and went back to where I was living with my friends, Ozelle and William. I lay there that night and got to thinking about that face. Then it dawned on me: that would probably be the way my mother would look in a nightclub. She'd never been to one. She'd be excited. She'd run back home and say, "Richard! Richard! Richard! I spoke to the star of the show!"

I couldn't sleep that night because I visualized my mother coming back, telling me that. Mom telling me, "I spoke to Harry Belafonte." I'd say, "No, Mom." She'd say, "Yes, he's going to call me."

Early Monday morning I called. I called with the feeling that I know the expression she's going to have on her face would be the same expression Mom would have on hers. And I could hear her expression in her voice, over the telephone. She was so excited. It was like I had called my mother.

This girl had looked so out of place in that nightclub. Sitting there, knowing that out of everybody in that nightclub, I asked for her number. She would look so out of place in a nightclub. So I talked with her and told her I would call her back and we'd have lunch. She was so excited it really made me feel just like I did when I was romping and stomping in my heyday. Nobody could stop me.

Summer rolled around. I worked hard, worked very hard. Then I went into the hospital about August with yellow jaundice. And

I never called Lillian anymore because I felt I wasn't good enough for her. The day I went to the hospital—I don't know—I called at her job because I wanted to let her know I was going to the hospital. It seemed that letting her know I was going was like letting my mother know. I called her and you would never realize I hadn't talked to her in a month. The concern. "Why hadn't you called?" Just like an excited little kid. I said, "I don't know if I'll stay, but here's my number at the house. You can call and find out."

They kept me lying there in that hospital, thinking about how hard I had worked, how I was going to miss being at work on the weekend. Then when my friends came and told me about the people that were at the club that weekend, how they missed me, how many of them were concerned—boy, that made me feel good. I never will forget that night. When the visitors left, I looked around and there was Lillian.

Something about the way she walked in. Because in the VA hospital, you can't bring anything up. She brought me Hershey bars, grapes, and I know she didn't slip them in.

She came in and I never had anybody in my life so concerned about me. When visiting hours were over, she asked if she could come back. I said, "No. It's so far over here."

She seemed so hurt, and I explained to her that it wasn't that. I said, "Yes, you can come. Bring me some books when you come back." She said, "Do you need anything?" I said, "Oh, yeah, some cigarette money."

Yeah, you lay in that hospital at night. I think that's what really made me do some real introspective thinking. Because I could gather myself. I could slow down for the first time and decide where I was going, where I was coming from. I lay there and thought about my college coach, and as I lay there in the hospital, for the first time in my life, I realized that I had found the one thing I was looking for. Show business. I had decided that I was going to go all the way in this thing.

I used to lie there and think and wait for visiting hours. It seemed like a coincidence that Lillian was always the last one to come by, because most of the people I knew were show business people, so they could get there without worrying to get off from work.

She came by that night, and I was really impressed with the type of books and magazines and things she brought me. It was the magazines I had always wanted to help keep me on top of the news, but I wasn't able to afford. *Life, Time, Look, Newsweek, Saturday Evening Post*, and *Reader's Digest*. And two cartons of cigarettes. I never had two cartons of cigarettes in my life. She opened up the drawer and put them in there, and she said, "I'm going to leave some cigarette money for you too." And I had asked her to bring me some small change for the telephone.

So we talked for a while. I never could find anything to say to her. She was a quiet and shy person, so we never talked too long. I'd tell her good night and tell her to go home before it was too late.

When I reached in the drawer to get a cigarette out, I remembered I had asked her to bring me some change for the telephone but—two rolls of quarters, paper money. I counted it: $100. I lay there and couldn't believe this because this was about the same way Mom would act. If Mom would have ever had any money, if I would ask her for anything, she would overdo it and still feel like she hadn't done enough.

I lay there and I couldn't believe this. I kind of had the feeling that all the hurt I thought I put Mom through, maybe Mom understood me better than I thought she did. Because the same thing this girl, Lillian, is doing for me would be the same thing my mother would do. I couldn't sleep that night for thinking about how Mom never had money in her pocketbook until I got sick, and she'd always bring in a dozen oranges, tell the kids not to eat it, it was for Richard. She'd bring in some soup. One good thing about being sick at my house, you got special food.

So when I got out of the hospital on a three-day pass, I took Lil to a movie. Taking her to a movie was like offering somebody the whole world. She couldn't believe it. So bashful and so shy.

About that time, Lil and I started dating pretty steady. Then again, not too much because she was so bashful. I really found myself lost for words on what to say. Then winter moved in and crowds were so full and lines so long, I said, "I've been here almost a year now and I guess it's time for me to get a raise—still making $10 a night." I walked up and asked the boss for a raise. He wouldn't give it to me, so I quit.

Had it pretty rough then. Staying home, watching television. People you thought you were a part of, you see them working every week, and you're not.

Then I had an idea. I heard someone say there was a nightclub called the Apex that was for sale. I called my good friend, Ira Murchison, and he came by with his car, carried me out there, and I talked to this lady. I talked to her and asked about a nightclub. She didn't know anything about owning the nightclub but told me she'd rent it to me for $56 a night. I didn't have two pennies in my pocket.

I told her okay. By this time, it's January of 1959; weather had broken nice, no snow on the ground. Nightclub was in Robbins, Illinois—about fifteen to twenty miles outside of Chicago. I knew I had to get into a nightclub where I could do the type of material I wanted to do. As great as I felt at the Esquire, it still was working to a big percentage of Guitar Red's audience. I felt if I went out there and got my own club, I'd have respect as a performer and respect as an owner. I'd have more leeway. My club. I wanted to see the customers treated a certain way. I knew if I made these customers comfortable, had the right atmosphere, I could get the type of comedy I wanted over.

So I went out there and while I was there this woman looked at Ira Murchison. She was an old woman, about seventy-something years old. She said, "You know you've been overseas and you're going back again." She was absolutely correct. Ira had actually been to a track meet in Moscow, and he had just returned to the States. I listened to this lady talk. Her name was Sally Wells. I heard her talking to Ira like I had heard women talk to my mother when she used to go and take me with her. I always used to hear my mother ask them, "Will Big Pres be back home? Will the kids be all right?" These women were fortune-tellers. I remember one time when I was about seven years old, one of these women looked at me and said, "You know, you don't believe in me, do you?" I didn't say anything because I didn't want to embarrass my mother, but I thought when people go to a spiritualist reader or fortune-teller it's pure ignorance.

This woman looked at me and she said, "You know." And then she looked at my mother and said, "He's going to be a great man one day. I see a star right in the center of his head." The woman said that when I was seven years old. I never forgot it. I never believed in them, but I never forgot that. I don't think it was what she said; it was the way she looked when she said it and the reaction my mother had.

Well, when I started running track, I thought this was what the woman meant. Now I'm sitting here in a place in 1959 and I see a woman by the name of Sally Wells talking to Ira Murchison the same way this woman used to talk to my mother. So I looked at her and I said, "Can you tell certain people things easier than you can other people?" She looked at me and said no, and she started talking to me.

It was January 1959. She said, "You know, I see you getting married."

I said, "Oh, you have to be in love first."

She said, "No, I see you getting married." She said, "I see you flying all over this country, from one end of it to the other, with a little brown case in your hand." And for some reason, I always felt that top comics always carried a little brown bag with their material in it. This really impressed me when she said that. She kept talking. She just smiled when she looked at me.

She rented me the club for $168 a week. I had a hard time keeping the club going, but I stayed there. All I had to pay was the band. Then I found out how beautiful it was having entertainers that drink heavy because some of the entertainers didn't have anything coming at the end of three days, they had drunk so much. I got to the point where I resented the entertainer who wasn't drinking because I had to pay him his full salary. I guess this is why I spend so much money in nightclubs today. Give them the salary back.

Then we started running into internal problems that all businesspeople have. I was bringing too much whiskey back to the guy who was letting me have it. By the end of January, I was keeping that nightclub open by getting a half pint of scotch, and a half pint of bourbon, a half pint of gin, and a half pint of vodka, and six cans of beer. And as I sold it, I would run across the street and get some more.

This was the true test. I was so far in debt I couldn't see straight.

And then to top this off, I had something happen to me that I wasn't expecting.

I called Lil and told her I needed some money. Well, when a girl comes to the hospital and brings you $100 and two rolls of quarters, and then gives you $800 to take care of expenses, you fail to realize that she's doing this just because she's so good inside. I thought she was rich, and I figured this was my ace in the hole.

I'll never forget, it was the last Thursday in January. I was out of the hospital and feeling good. I was back in business. Money was tight so I went by to see Lil, and that's when I got the news.

She said, "I can give you $300, but I've quit my job and I'm leaving town." I asked her why. She said, "I'm pregnant."

I said, "Really?" Yeah, I couldn't believe it. The last thing in the world I needed was a baby.

I sat and I talked. I knew this was it. At that point I had to weigh something. I had to weigh this. I was brought up in a home with no daddy in it, and as good and as ornery and as dirty and as rotten as my daddy was, he gave us a last name. Knowing I'm in no shape to get married, knowing I didn't want a kid to have to go under the conditions I had to go under, and to top that off not have a name, I asked her would she marry me, and she said no. She said I was working too hard and she wouldn't do anything to be in my way. I insisted that she marry me.

I never will forget what Old Lady Wells told me the first week in January. She said, "You'll be getting married soon." Lil broke the news to me on Thursday, the last Thursday in January. Friday, we got the blood tests, bought the license, and Monday, the second of February 1959, I was a married man.

I explained to her what we had to go through. I sent her down to

St. Louis. That same night we got married, we got on a Greyhound bus and went to St. Louis. First time I'd been back home since I'd left. And here I was bringing a strange woman to live with some strange people.

By that time, my sisters and them had moved. We got to St. Louis. That was a funny day down there. It sleeted. Got in town that morning, the buses weren't running. The insurance companies had issued orders that anybody that would drive their car wouldn't be covered. No cabs. Got off that bus. Couldn't even walk. Just so happened there was a guy bootlegging. He took us to my sister's house.

It was a horrible experience for Lil because I was taking her someplace I hadn't been myself. I carried her there, and then I had to run by and see all my kinfolks and this and that. Then I had to get right back up to Chicago. I told her everything would be all right because the nightclub had to break for me. She stayed. At this point she didn't have a quarter. She had to buy the ring and the license.

I went back to the nightclub, and it seemed the harder I would work the worse the weather would get. Do you know what it feels like to stay in a nightclub for six months and never walk out of there, not one night, with a dollar bill that's your own? Six months I stayed there and never walked out with a dollar bill that was mine.

The bad weather lasted all the way through March and April. It broke a little bit in May, but by that time I had such bad credit, I couldn't even advertise. Just a few stragglers that knew I was there would come out.

One night something happened to me in that club. One night in May I had about six people in the club all night. I was doing miracle work because I had a wife down in St. Louis that I had never been able to send a quarter to the whole time she was there. I couldn't even call up on the phone anymore because my phone bill had run up so high they cut it off. I hadn't paid any rent to the people I was living with in so long, then I turned around and got their phone cut off, plus I got them into debt.

But I had to keep that nightclub open. I would cry when Friday would roll around. I would go everywhere I could to borrow money, till I couldn't borrow money anymore. All my friends lent me every penny they could get their hands on. The waitresses had never been paid from the time I carried them out there until the time I closed my door. They never complained because they had faith in me. I told them every night, "Next week has got to be the week." It's impossible to be in the nightclub business five months and never make a penny. I couldn't believe it. I'd never believe it. But it happened.

Then that first week in May a guy pulled a gun out in the club. I'm working under the pressure now that the baby's going to be born in May and the club's got to hit. I don't want my baby born in a city hospital. When the guy pulled that gun out, I walked right over to him and looked him in the eye. "Mister, you don't know what I've been through." People were jumping up and running out. I said, "I guess one of us has to die tonight. What I've gone through in this place here, you need to pull a gun on me to run me out here. God himself couldn't run me out." He turned around and said he was sorry and walked out.

I didn't want my baby born in a city hospital, so I arranged with a doctor I knew to have Lil sent to a private hospital. When I got home, I was surprised to see Lil there. She said, "Michele was born here on the floor. Greg, when I lay here, I guess the reason I couldn't holler at the hospital, I was so proud that your son was going to be born. When I found out it was a girl, I thought you would be mad at me. I didn't know she was a girl until they told me at the hospital."

I just said, "Well."

She kept talking, "I laid here, Greg, and your sister asked me why I didn't cry and holler. I felt so good. And when it really dawned on me what happened I sit on this floor and I thought, 'Not too bad.' Dick Gregory's kid stands on the corner and says, 'Dick Gregory's my daddy.' He will never say, 'I was born on the floor.' He'll say, 'Dick Gregory's my daddy.' Greg, you can do anything you want to do. You know that, and I know that. Don't let nothing stop you."

I said, "You know, I'm thinking about quitting show business." Hell, I'm nothing but a peon then. Haven't worked in a big nightclub. Only been in one once and that was to see the show. Haven't been able to afford to go back to that one again. She said, "Greg, I get lonely here without you and I cry a lot. I hear your sister telling you, you ought to quit that. Greg, for me and Michele, don't ever quit what you believe in—what you want to do. The things you told me about your mother. If she could do all those things for six of you, I can do anything you want me to do. I understand you can't always come down here. I look for you every day. When the day is gone and the week is gone, I just keeping seeing you coming. I know you're on the way."

I stayed there three days. Left and went back to Chicago and opened up the club. It's June now. Easter Sunday was a good Sunday. The place was packed. I made just enough money for me to decide this place was going to hit now. Suffered through the whole storm and now the weather broke. Forgot about my back rent.

Well, crowds started coming in, and a couple of people started wanting the club. Lady told me. She was nice to me. My license, heat, water bill, taxes. Kinda broke my heart that I had taken a ghost that had been closed up for years, opened it up, and held those doors open through one of the worst winters in Chicago. Now I have to have four months' rent in: $56 a night, times three nights a week times four times four. "Has to be in by Sunday, Mr. Gregory."

I can say one thing—track had really helped me because I went out like a champ and like a star. Sort of like seeing the buzzards come in that weekend, looking the place over. Looking at the crowd. Wondering how they were going to decorate it. Could have been a real bitter pill to take, to keep a club open all the winter, in all the rain, and now have to give it up. That Sunday night we threw a party. People were sad, people had worked there for six months with no pay, and they cried, because every Friday, Saturday, and Sunday they could look forward to being somebody—being a part of a thing—ethical, honest. They looked forward to someone saying, "Excuse me, Miss." Looked forward to coming to work in a place where the customer was going to be treated right and the help was going to be treated right. That meant more than money to those people, and the last night I took the money and split it with them.

I will never forget when I walked down those steps for the last time and I thought about how many trails I had made across the street, how many friends I had made, and no one would ever be able to say there was gambling (which I had been offered), prostitution (which I had been offered), or hot whiskey. Because of the church structure of that nightclub, I always called it a church. If God was in as many churches as he was in that nightclub with me, this would be a better world. That was my church. That is where I learned to live my final lesson before I hit: I learned how to treat people. With all the bitterness that I had to come through, if I would have hit where I am now without that period, I might have been working with the power structure against the people.

I had a very special lesson there. When I walked down those steps for the last time. I looked at the people that walked out that were sad and I said, "You know, you people have really been changed. If you kept your eyes open wide, you would have watched a boy grow into a man. You carry fifty pounds of ice; if you don't weaken, you strengthen your back to carry a hundred pounds. If you don't weaken, you strengthen it to carry a thousand. Before you know it, you pick up all the ice in the world and haul it." That's how strong I felt.

Nobody could lend me their nightclub to practice the kind of stuff I wanted to practice. The average Black man at that nightclub had never heard anything but the blue material.

No other place could I have worked for six months and developed what I had developed there under the pressure that I was under. And when I hit my last step, I said, "I'm ready now. Goodbye, Apex. Goodbye, Apex. And thank you so much. I learned a lot. And I'll not be turning back now."

I'm out of work again. No money. When I split the money, I didn't keep a dime. From July to September, I looked for a job and I never found one. My baby was born in May. Between May and September, I was never able to scrape up bus fare to go to St. Louis and see her. Then one day I got so disgusted I just got downright ornery and evil, and embarrassed. I called Lil, after not being able to call her for two weeks. And I said, "Baby, come home. I made up my mind that it might be a little bit easier if you were here watching me starve."

As much as this woman loved me, and as bad as she wanted to be with me, for some reason she told me, "That's okay, Greg. I don't want to come to Chicago. Not right now." I couldn't believe it. I hung up and I went back out and I looked and I looked. It's a horrible feeling to go through all the things I'd gone through, and I was about ready to take a job shining shoes.

It's August now, and I go back to my old nightclub where they gave me $10 a night, and when I got there I asked for a $2 raise. Yep. I'm right back at that same nightclub. Same nightclub where I started at $10 a night. It seemed like twenty years ago. That's how much I had gone through. I couldn't believe that just a little while ago I had walked up and asked for a $2 raise and he wouldn't give it to me so I quit. I knew I could get other gigs, and I did.

NO BUSINESS LIKE SHOW BUSINESS

"I'M ALL RIGHT"

It's 1960. That year I made $1,500 the whole year. I averaged out $30 a week. I went back into Roberts Show Club and stayed a long time this time. I was really proud of myself at Roberts. The first time I had ever invited Lil, Sammy Davis came in with Nipsey Russell. When Nipsey came in, he was the comic and I was just the emcee. When Sammy Davis came in, that's when I learned one of my greatest lessons in show business. It was the cause of me making it in three years instead of thirty.

Sammy Davis and Nipsey Russell were the biggest attraction that Roberts ever had in his show club. Being that Roberts had to pay me anyway, after he tried to tell me that I was laid off while they were there, I told him he should let me emcee even though Nipsey was the comic. So they found things for me to do while I was waiting, like help seat people.

I guess the whole time Sammy was there he drew a 95 percent white audience. For some of them it was the first time they'd ever been to the South Side. For some it was the first time they'd ever been to the South Side at night. The place seats almost fifteen hundred people and it's packed, all the way up to the back door. White people are paying something like $50 tips to get a seat close to the front.

Nipsey opened up the show, and he slayed them. I couldn't believe it. Sammy came on with all of his talents, but you could truly say that Nipsey Russell stole that show. I couldn't understand why. And when I did learn this lesson, it was the thing that made me hit it in show business.

I called my wife that night, and I said I'm looking at something that's so strange here. Nipsey Russell is one of the funniest men in show business, and Sammy is the most talented in show business and there's no comparison. And yet Nipsey is stealing this show.

Well, at the Chez Paree they had what they called AGVA [American Guild of Variety Artists] night. On Monday nights, all of the acts in the AGVA union can go and perform in this big nightclub, and nightclub owners come in and look at the talent. I had gone down many times, not knowing that Black comedians weren't accepted in white places. The union people kept asking me, "Don't you dance? Don't you sing?" They told me the first spot that would be open for a comedian was about a year and a half off. Knowing what they meant by it, I didn't bother them anymore.

Nipsey went over so well at Roberts they decided to bring him down for AGVA night. I went down, and Nipsey opened up with racial jokes and nobody laughed. He sat there and died, compared to the response of the white people the night before. That was the key to the whole comic problem in America. A white man will come to a Black nightclub and he's so afraid and so nervous that anything you mention about race, it just knocks him out. The harder he laughs, the more that means, "I'm all right." But when Nipsey got downtown, where the white man wasn't in Nipsey's house but in his own, the white man didn't want to hear that and he didn't laugh. That was the difference.

Nipsey overshadowed Sammy Davis at Roberts—a Black club in a Black neighborhood—because this was definitely guilt and fear of this neighborhood. Of the Black waitress that had to wait on him. Of the Black guy at the door who took his money. So when Nipsey mentioned racial things, whitey felt very uncomfortable and he laughed. And he laughed and he laughed. If a white man's sitting in a Black place and a waitress drops a drink on him, he'll jump up and say, "Excuse me." In a white joint, the club might have a lawsuit. So after I figured this out, I knew which way to go and I started working on it.

Then I realized at one point there was going to be an insult. Some white guy in a white club was going to call me "nigger." Every white person in the club was going to be embarrassed. This created a hell of a problem, because if a white man brings me in his nightclub and I get insulted and customers walk out, they will remember the incident and tie it to that nightclub. Then it actually would be better for this white man to keep me out of his club. I saw the parallel with when I was kicked in the mouth as a little boy shining shoes. If a customer calls me a nigger in a nightclub, the owner is in the same situation as that bartender—losing customers over me.

I started developing a comeback, and for six months, I had Lil yell insults at me. For some reason, I wasn't getting the answer. A split second of thinking could mean I would lose the whole crowd. Once it happened, people would start feeling sorry for me. And if someone feels sorry for me, I can't make them laugh after I recover. Comedy is no more than disappointment with a friendly relation. A man cannot have relations toward another man when he feels sorry for him. An example: If you give money to a blind person, you don't have a friendly relationship with him. If you think so, let him tell you that what you gave him isn't enough. Your mother could tell you it wasn't enough, and you wouldn't get mad. But with the blind man, you would. You don't have a friendly attitude toward him; you have a sympathetic attitude.

So I've got to figure a way out. One night, I was out of work, hadn't been out of the house in about four days because I didn't have any money, and there were about thirteen inches of snow. I was lying on the couch and looked across at Lil. Bitter at the whole world, nobody to pick on but her, I said, "What would you do if from here on in I started referring to you as 'bitch'?" She jumped out of the chair and said, "I would simply ignore you."

I fell out of the couch and laughed so hard they had to call a doctor 'cause I was bleeding inside. That was the answer that I wanted in a nightclub. That quick, sophisticated answer, with no bitterness. That way I wouldn't give the audience time to feel sorry for me. Once I had this, I'm ready.

I went into a very unsophisticated white club on the outskirts of town, in a neighborhood where I'm dealing with the factory worker whose only mark of dignity is to be the foreman over "that nigger," and can get away from him on the weekend. Then one night it happened. A guy called me a nigger and the audience froze. I wheeled around without batting an eye and said, "Did you hear what that guy just called me? Roy Rogers's horse 'Trigger'!" I hit them so quick and so fast that they laughed, because this is what they wanted to believe he had said. Now that I had them locked up completely on my side, I said, "My contract reads that every time I hear that word, I get $50 more a night. So would everybody in the room stand up and yell it?"

Then I got a job in Mishawaka, Indiana, for $10 a night. The white people lined up at eight o'clock to see this thing. On a Saturday night, a group of white girls were sitting over in the lounge chairs far back to my left. One of them yelled out, "You're handsome." Every white man in that place froze. The sex angle was thrown right in my face, and they could hate me for it. I looked at the girl and said, "Honey, what nationality are you?" She said, "Hungarian." I said, "Take another drink and you'll think you're Black, and you'll run up here and kiss me and we'll both have to leave this town in a hurry." I got myself and the nightclub owner off the spot. I left there feeling pretty good because I had tested a white audience with the type of things I wanted to use.

THE CHICAGO PLAYBOY CLUB

An entertainer named Irwin Corey refused to work a Sunday night at the Playboy Club. My agent, Freddie Williamson, got me in there for $50. I never will forget it. It was very cold out, and I didn't know that much about the Loop. I borrowed a quarter carfare from the people downstairs. That just shows you how amazing life is. For the biggest job I ever had in my life, I had to borrow a quarter. For the job that made me, that skyrocketed me to $5,000 a week, it seems like you would have to borrow $1,000, but it was just a quarter separating me from one of the biggest things that would ever happen to me.

I got on the bus, but not knowing the right way, I had to walk about twenty blocks to the Playboy. It was like when I was a kid, where I'd get so cold on my paper route the wind would knock the water out of my eyes. I am almost frozen by the time I get to the door, and when I walked up, they gave me the news: "We're sorry, but you can't go on. This room has been sold out to a southern frozen food convention, and we didn't know it." I think had I not been so cold and so mad, I probably could have accepted it, but after that walk, I explained to the room manager that nothing short of death itself would keep me from going on.

It's one thing having local yokels, the poor whites of Chicago, heckle you. It's another thing having the businessman, the man that's spending top dollar, a man that's been around. An audience that, when it's all over, you can't say, "These are ignorant white folks."

As I sat there on that stage, I went all the way back to childhood. To the smile Mom had on her face, to the clever way of being so bitter inside but smiling on the outside, when your rent wasn't paid and you knew they were going to cut you off, when the lights were cut off but you could see in the dark. I went through all of this sitting up there on that stage, and when it was all over, I smiled.

The audience fought me and with their dirty little insulting statements. I would accept it and say something very clever back, to the extent where they broke. And when they broke, it was like the storm was over. They turned around, and they looked, and they listened. What was supposed to be a fifteen-minute show lasted an hour and ten minutes. They didn't let me off. Every time I tried to get off, they called me back. When I finally walked off the stage, these southerners stood up and clapped. One of them looked at me and said, "You know, if you have the right managers, you'll die a billionaire."

Working the Playboy Club, I had figured out the solution to this whole problem of cracking the top white nightclubs. I wasn't broke nowhere but in my pocket.

BREAKTHROUGH

INTERVIEW WITH MIKE WALLACE (APRIL 10, 1961)

During his first nightclub engagement in New York City, in the midst of his meteoric rise following his breakthrough at Chicago's Playboy Club, Gregory sat down with journalist Mike Wallace for his first prime-time network television interview.

WALLACE: Dick, in a matter of just a few months you've joined the ranks of America's top "egghead" comics. Your trademark is finding humor in the serious and often tragic problems of your race. What memories of your personal experiences do you carry with you from your early days growing up in St. Louis?

GREGORY: We were poor economically, but rich in humor. Coming up on relief, and then having the type of humorous mother that I had, there were certain things we looked forward to when we were kids. We knew the lights were going to be cut off every so often. Anytime they were on past that time, it was just a matter that they hadn't got around to our house yet. Mom would walk in, or we'd meet her at the streetcar from work and tell her, "The lights are off! The lights are off!" You know, this was a big thing. She would always tell us, "Well, this is what it looks like behind the moon."

And we found out years later when Russia made the first shot that it's black behind the moon!

WALLACE: How many youngsters were there in your family?

GREGORY: Six of us.

WALLACE: And your mother supported the family?

GREGORY: She supported us.

WALLACE: And you were on relief for a good long time?

GREGORY: All the way until 1950.

WALLACE: A totally segregated neighborhood?

GREGORY: Yeah, totally segregated neighborhood that we lived in.

WALLACE: So you didn't know—or did you know—a good deal about racial prejudice?

GREGORY: No, we couldn't find it out too much. You have a lot of cities up north that are so cut up we don't worry about segregated schools as long as you have segregated neighborhoods. It was a pressure we never actually come in close contact with. You could duck racial prejudice at home, in an indirect way, for about ten years before you knew. The only whites you'd come in contact with were the ones in the neighborhood, and they were the best people in the world because they make their living on you, on the Negro in the neighborhood.

WALLACE: So they were kind of nice to you?

GREGORY: Yes, the only white people you'd come into immediate contact with were the nice ones.

WALLACE: You once said, "School was the only place where I could be hurt." What did you mean by that?

GREGORY: I had an incident happen to me when I was about seven years old, when they were taking up money for the community chest. And at this time, I wasn't aware that we were poor and on relief. I knew a big truck pulled up to the house, and I thought this was something to be proud of. This was dignity, you know, we won't come get it, you bring it to us! They were taking up this money for the community chest. On a Friday the teacher would ask, "How much will your father pledge to send Monday?" I'd always been working. I was in the taverns when I was five years old shining shoes, or washing cars, or selling papers. I had some money, so this was one day that I was going to buy me a daddy. The teacher said, "How much will your father send?" Things were very tough for everybody, so when I stood up and said $15, well, this was unheard of. The teacher looked at me and said, "You know, we're taking up this money for you and your kind, and if you can afford to give this much money to the community chest, you don't need to be on relief."

WALLACE: Oh, my.

GREGORY: This caught me by surprise, and not until then was I aware that we were poor. So then I felt that school was a place where I could be hurt.

WALLACE: Oh, I can understand that. Were you in St. Louis during the very tense period when the public swimming pools were being desegregated?

GREGORY: Yes, the one where we had the big trouble was at Fairgrounds Park. I use it in my act. "All our parents made us get out there whether you could swim or not. They were nice to us because they knew they had to integrate, so they hired a new lifeguard for us. But he was blind. We all walked out to this integrated swimming pool on this glorious day, diving board, fifty feet in the air, we got up and jumped. And they drained the pool."

WALLACE: You went to Southern Illinois University?

GREGORY: Right.

WALLACE: Who helped to put you through school? Yourself?

GREGORY: I had a scholarship in track. I ran the mile and the half mile.

WALLACE: Oh, really?

GREGORY: I'd won the state championship.

WALLACE: You had an athletic scholarship, and you majored in business administration, but you left school before graduation. How come?

GREGORY: I don't know. Just something that hit me one night. It seemed like I wasn't doing what I really wanted to do.

WALLACE: How old are you now?

GREGORY: Twenty-eight.

WALLACE: After you left school, you got a job in a Chicago post office, but I understand that your sense of humor cost you your job. How come?

GREGORY: Well, the post office struck me as being so amusing. It looked like all the postal help had been there fifteen and twenty years, and about the only satisfaction they got out of coming to work was to find a newly hired employee putting an airmail letter in the wrong box. And I loved to do this because it looked like this gave them new life. With racial pressure in this country, I found a lot of humor and a lot of comedy in it. So in the post office, anytime I found a letter going to Mississippi, I put it in the foreign box. It was humor to me. If it had been bitterness, I probably would have torn it up or destroyed it or something.

WALLACE: How do you account for the fact that you were able to escape all vestige of bitterness? Or have you escaped all of that?

GREGORY: There's been so many problems that we would laugh at. You take a situation we had in 1958, when they raised the three-cent stamp to the four-cent stamp, and people in certain areas in the South said, "We don't want a four-cent stamp with Abraham Lincoln's picture on it." But they wouldn't get rid of his $5 bills. This strikes me as being very funny. The whole racial idea—if you just twist it around backwards—we portray the Indian in this country as being savage. We invaded his land and all he was doing was fighting for his land. It's the same thing as if I break into your home. If I can overpower you and win, this is one thing. But why come out five years later and paint him being the savage, when I broke into your home and ran off with your property?

WALLACE: That's right.

I don't mean to ask you to do your entire act for us at these prices, but nonetheless, would you care to make some comments on the news? Tell me how you put this stuff together. Do you write your own material?

GREGORY: Oh, I never write it. It's just a matter of looking at the newspapers and you find it. This week there has been so much going on. We have a situation going in Cuba [the aftermath of the Bay of Pigs invasion]. I don't believe it's as big as it is. I can see where good propaganda would make it seem so. In other words, if you had three men walk into your house, and after you beat up the three and had everything under control, you holler out the window saying, "There's fifty guys in here!" Well, this makes you look greater, and I feel the same thing is happening there. So I just twist it and say, "They probably have bigger fights in Xavier Cugat's band." It's just a matter of twisting it. You take Miami. It's one of the few cities where you go down and shake a tree, and six oranges and seven Cubans will fall to the ground. These are the situations you see in the newspaper. You had the Russian that just made it to outer space, which is a wonderful thing. Then you read where you become weightless. He couldn't feel his hands, he couldn't feel his legs, and he floated out of his chair. He said he could write, but he had to hold the pad. Well, I get like that two and three times a week, and it doesn't cost this country $2 billion. This is the humor that I see.

WALLACE: What's the difference between racial prejudice in the North and South?

GREGORY: It's actually no difference. In the South, they don't care how close I get, as long as I don't get too big. And up north, they don't care how big I get, as long as I don't get too close.

WALLACE: What are your thoughts on some nonracial topics? Like President Kennedy.

GREGORY: Well, you have to realize one thing. This is the first president we've ever elected in the history of this country that moved into a smaller house.

WALLACE: The Bureau of Internal Revenue, now that you're in the higher income tax bracket?

GREGORY: Yeah, that's why I smoke so much. I write off about 180 cartons a year on my income tax, and they haven't found a way to get around that. But they told me every time they see me, I better be smoking.

WALLACE: Tell me this, Dick. Until how recently, I mean this quite seriously, was money a problem for you?

GREGORY: Up until a month ago. Last year, the whole year in entertainment, I think I cleared about $1,500.

WALLACE: In all of 1960, you made $1,500? An average of about $30 a week?

GREGORY: Yep.

WALLACE: And in 1961 your income will be what, do you figure?

GREGORY: From what I've been reading in the paper, they said everything from $500,000 to $800,000, on the assumption that the record takes off and goes as big as they expect.

WALLACE: From $1,500 to $500,000 in one year. Have you ever tried to analyze why this happened?

GREGORY: I don't think you can. I've always believed that if you do what you want to do, and work hard at what you believe in, you'll never get cheated.

WALLACE: But there must be something special in Dick Gregory that, at this time in 1961, suddenly made people latch on to you.

GREGORY: I really couldn't say. It might have happened last year or the year before. It's just the right timing, being at the right place at the right time. The biggest break I had was at the Playboy Club filling in for a comic in Chicago. There was a convention in town, and the room was filled with southerners. I've always believed that my act would go with southerners, because as long as you're telling the truth, regardless of how bad it hurts . . .

WALLACE: You played the first time out to a roomful of southerners? What happened?

GREGORY: I was supposed to go on for fifteen minutes, and they kept me on the stage for an hour and ten minutes.

WALLACE: My golly. And there was no bitterness?

GREGORY: I had a little bit of heckling at the beginning, but once you can handle the hecklers and just stay right on them . . .

WALLACE: When you first tried to get a job with the kind of jokes that you do in Chicago, I would imagine it was kind of tough?

GREGORY: It was tough trying to get a job simply because you can't start off in show business in the top nightclubs. And when you are very topical, and talking about touchy problems, you have to be in the range to reach the man between the eight to fifteen thousand a year bracket. They think differently. They've read the same books. I tell jokes about the Mann Act. Everybody in the nightclubs I'm working now, they've heard about the Mann Act. Telling jokes about Kennedy, I don't use the word *Harvard*. I use the word *Cambridge*, and all these people understand. Whereas in the lower nightclubs, in the neighborhood places, this is where you're at a loss with topical material and trying to keep it at their level. There are a lot of touchy things that, just by wording it in a certain way, it will go over.

WALLACE: You must be a happy fellow?

GREGORY: I'm very happy.

WALLACE: I can understand. Thanks, Richard, for coming and spending this time.

GREGORY: My pleasure.

INTERVIEW WITH PAUL KRASSNER, *THE REALIST* (SEPTEMBER 1961)

Gregory was the subject of numerous newspaper and magazine profiles in his first year on the national scene. The most unconventional, and perhaps the most revealing, was a featured interview in Paul Krassner's renegade satirical publication The Realist.

KRASSNER: How do you feel about always being referred to as a Negro comedian?

GREGORY: I have no feelings about it one way or the other.

KRASSNER: I mean in terms of a label. Lenny Bruce would never be introduced on TV as a Caucasian comedian. In other words, how do you feel about being singled out by color?

GREGORY: It's just something we're up against, and we've been up against, and we've learned to accept it and live with it. Because we're the only ones you *wouldn't* need to say this about. You don't have to say, "Jackie Robinson is a Negro baseball player," unless you're blind.

KRASSNER: Do you think it would be kind of a sign of total integration if you could be, say, as offensive as Lenny Bruce without feeling you had any special responsibility not to be?

GREGORY: Oh, I think I could be just as offensive as Lenny Bruce. It's just a matter of your personality makeup.

KRASSNER: I'm thinking of a review in the *San Francisco Examiner*.

Dick Nolan wrote that it helps that you are "likable as a person," which you wouldn't be, he says, if you "had the compulsive urge to shock that is Lenny Bruce's forte."

GREGORY: Well, this is just a guy that doesn't like Lenny Bruce. I mean he would probably say the same thing about Bob Hope against Lenny Bruce.

KRASSNER: It seems to me you've cut down on the proportion of racial humor in your act. Why is that?

GREGORY: Because it's not as topical. Even when I started, I'd say 90 percent of the act was topical. At the time when I hit it big, every time you'd pick up the paper, for a period of nine months, a Black man was in the headlines—either in the Congo situation, or aggravated school situation, or in some form or another.

KRASSNER: What newspapers and magazines do you read?

GREGORY: All of them. Every one I get my hands on.

KRASSNER: Is it true that you have a $1,200-a-month phone bill?

GREGORY: Oh, sure, because I make phone calls all over the country to find out different things. Last night I made about eight calls to find out the effects of the Dag Hammarskjöld thing. It was very frightening. I mean, I know some people that really didn't dig him and they'd love to see him out of there, but not that way.

KRASSNER: You try to keep up with the headlines in your performances, but with a tragedy like this . . .

GREGORY: You go back and you knock it out. I knocked out everything about the Congo and everything about airplanes. You just knock it out altogether.

KRASSNER: When you were just getting started, you had all-Negro audiences. Now, from what I've seen, you have almost 100 percent white audiences. Has your material changed in the process?

GREGORY: This is automatic. I can go in a white man's club and do an act for twenty minutes on my stocks and bonds. Can't do it in a Negro nightclub. Shelley Berman made a million talking about "coffee, tea, or milk" on the airplane, but how many Negroes have you seen on an airplane compared to whites? So you would do your routine about trains and buses. This is an automatic thing, from the economic standpoint. You can get on a million subjects in a white nightclub that you couldn't hardly touch in a predominantly Negro nightclub. How could I do a takeoff on the Metropolitan Opera at a Negro nightclub? Or a Broadway play? How many Negroes have been to New York to see this Broadway play? Whereas in a white nightclub, any place in the country, you can assume they've been there or have read the reviews. If I do a takeoff on expense accounts in a Negro nightclub, I'm dead.

KRASSNER: Bernard Wolfe wrote in an essay, in a book called *The Scene Before You*, that "by a devious racial irony the 'creative' Negro, far from being his own spontaneous self, may actually be dramatizing the white man's image of the 'spontaneous' Negro 'as he really is.'" Do you think this applies to your style? For example, Dickson Terry, a correspondent for the *St. Louis Post-Dispatch*, wrote that you approach the microphone with "a sort of Stepin Fetchit expression" on your face; and Bob Rolontz, a reviewer for *Billboard*, said that you occasionally use "a semi-dialect that is not necessary."

GREGORY: This is *me*. See, a white man—and I'm so goddamn sick and tired of a white man telling *us* about *us*—he can't. He tells us, "Wait, take your time." You can't tell me to wait. You're not Black twenty-four hours a day. You don't have any right to tell me to wait on racial equality. I have the right to tell you I'm willing. But you don't have the right—if I'm bleeding, and another person's bleeding. I have the right to say, "This fellow's hurt worse than I am, let him go first." You don't have the right to tell me this.

And this is the right that the white man has been assuming for years: that he knows more about us than we know about ourselves. And this is wrong. He knows about us what we want him to know. He never follows us home.

We know more about him than he knows about us. He does things around us *because* we don't count that his friends know nothing about. But what the critics say, it's because it makes good print. I talk the way *I* wanna talk.

KRASSNER: Obviously, then, when you use a double negative on stage, or when you say "mizzuble" instead of "miserable," you're not patronizing the audience.

GREGORY: No. I *talk* like this. Check Southern Illinois University, you'll find out. It's just me, period. I'm not trying to prove nothing to no one. The bank president doesn't care how I say it, long as I get it in there.

KRASSNER: A friend of mine wrote to Liebmann Breweries and asked how come they never had any Negroes as contestants in the Miss Rheingold contest; now Schaefer beer, on the other hand, seems to slant toward the Negro market in particular.

GREGORY: We have this dual advertising, where one company will advertise on the Negro side of town, which I don't go along with at all. I hate it.

KRASSNER: What's your policy about being booked at clubs in the southern states?

GREGORY: Every Negro in show business should take a position not to perform to a segregated audience.

KRASSNER: But you would perform in the South to an integrated audience?

GREGORY: They'd have to pass new laws just for me to get in there.

KRASSNER: What's your attitude toward playing overseas?

GREGORY: Right now I'm debating. I wouldn't feel right doing my act in London when I know I couldn't do it in Mississippi. That makes it have a propaganda aspect.

KRASSNER: Wouldn't it be nice if someday I could interview you without asking a single question about race?

GREGORY: I couldn't care less.

KRASSNER: Incidentally, I was supposed to interview you a few days ago, but I understand you flew to Chicago. If it's not too personal, could I ask why?

GREGORY: To see my family. I have a little baby daughter that's six weeks old, and that's the only time I can get home because my schedule never breaks.

KRASSNER: Have you found that being a financial success has changed you in any way other than that you can afford to be with your family like that?

GREGORY: Sure, it changes you in every way. Last year I could've called a guy a dirty son of a bitch. I do it this year, I got a lawsuit against me.

PART II

THE MIND

(1961–1970)

After surviving his difficult childhood and teenage years, Dick Gregory was a far cry from 1803 North Taylor. He promised his mother that no Gregory would ever live on North Taylor again, and he planned to see that through. Determined to keep his word, he excelled. The funny man from the South Side was now one of the biggest names in show business. Fatherhood clearly changed his lens. He was a loving, doting dad— all daughters at this point—and he couldn't have been happier. He reshaped his paternal DNA in one generation. He was a change agent, devastating glass ceilings. From The Tonight Show's couch to the halls of Congress, Dick Gregory had become a force to be reckoned with.

—CHRISTIAN GREGORY

CONGRESSIONAL TESTIMONY ON DISCRIMINATION IN THE PERFORMING ARTS

(October 30, 1962)

In the fall of 1962, Dick Gregory made his first appearance on Broadway as part of a month-long revue featuring singer Eddie Fisher and dancer Juliet Prowse. While the comedian was embraced on "the Great White Way," Gregory was eager to help other Black performers by testifying before a congressional committee—chaired by the powerful Adam Clayton Powell of Harlem—investigating the impact of racism in the entertainment industry. His testimony followed positive accounts on the opportunities for Black entertainers by producers, directors, and entertainment industry executives.

POWELL: I would like to state that these are just exploratory talks, that the whole matter will be gone into in much more detail by the subcommittee which I shall appoint in January. We will hold hearings of that committee in various sections of the United States . . .

I shall now ask Mr. Gregory to come forward. Mr. Gregory is a very busy man and I know he has to leave. I kept your name yesterday, Mr. Gregory. You said you did not object to the "Longest

Day" being all white, but that you insisted there be a subtitle, "This portrays a segregated regiment."

GREGORY: It is a pleasure being here.

I walked in late, but from the testimony I heard, I can't see what the hearings are being held for. It seems like all the Negroes are working, but really, after these meetings are over, you should go out and look into it yourself. It will be very simple.

POWELL: We had ample testimony yesterday, contradicting what has been said here today, from actors, and we are sure from your own experience, you can give evidence, as you just have, that there is plenty of discrimination.

GREGORY: The only TV show that hires Negroes regularly is the Saturday night boxing. After that, we can forget about it.

POWELL: And Puerto Ricans?

GREGORY: Yes.

I don't know. I can't speak for myself, as far as racial discrimination goes, in television, because I am more comfortable myself in a nightclub, making social comments. You have to take into consideration that you have in television a mass medium with 20 or 30 million people listening who may not have the proper educational level to grasp what you are saying, so I find more leeway in a nightclub.

I almost would not hesitate to take a census of where 90 percent of that would fall.

POWELL: That is the first time this has been brought up.

GREGORY: We cannot even advertise Cadillacs. As far as movies and certain roles on television are concerned, I heard certain people don't write any Negro parts. I would like to know who would have to write me a Negro part? I have been one all my life. If you give me the part of a doctor to play, I will make him a Negro. I can't do anything else, but I think a lot of research should go into this because this is a very touchy thing.

It is a point where all minority groups are getting tired of this. The only time you ever see Negroes in a movie is in a jail scene or in a Communist rally. I don't think anybody would have an objection to the "Untouchables" showing a Negro scientist or something like that.

Down through the years, the Chinese have always been portrayed as Charlie Chan or a simple Chinese detective. How can you explain to an American kid that the Chinese are a world power because we have always shown the negative side?

They say, "There are a lot of things you can't do on television today," and minority groups are being blamed for this—that we are touchy.

Years ago you heard of Stepin Fetchit and all these Negro actors playing the kind of roles they had to play, but we did not frown on that. A lot of minority groups have made a mistake in grumping about that. We did not frown on it. Stepin Fetchit got top billing with Bob Hope.

Years ago the stomach was hungry; today the stomach is no longer hungry, but the mind is hungry. At that time we had to be easily satisfied. Today they aren't satisfied in their minds so easily.

Hollywood made a great mistake years ago, during Hitler's time. They should have known how the mass medium affects people in different sections of the world. How can you show "Naked City" with no Negroes involved? How can you show anything with no Negroes involved? The response is: "We would do it, but we would lose customers."

POWELL: Ed Sullivan this morning testified that that is totally untrue; that Negro performers on his show have not met with any reaction at all, except in increased car sales. The advertising agencies are lying, the producers are lying, and Ed Sullivan's testimony proves it.

GREGORY: Ed Sullivan's show is an exceptional case.

I have to take my hat off to Jack Paar because Jack Paar used sophisticated Negroes on his show, more than just an entertainer or a performer, and I think his show played a great part in the acceptance of minority groups.

I ask myself: What is the difference between a Governor Barnett in Mississippi taking the stand that he decided to take to save his face with his Mississippi friends, and the "Huntley-Brinkley Report" being afraid to lose their customers? I ask myself: What is the difference between a General Walker and these other shows?

It has come to a point now where someone has to get into it, the Federal Government, or someone, because all this affects the Federal Government.

INTERVIEW WITH RALPH GLEASON, KPFA RADIO

(May 25, 1963)

Gregory's first direct participation in civil rights activities took place in Greenwood, Mississippi. In February 1963, he personally delivered several tons of food to poor Leflore County residents who were cut off from the public surplus commodities program because of a voter registration campaign organized by the Student Nonviolent Coordinating Committee (SNCC). A few months later, he joined their marches on the county courthouse, in which Black citizens challenged local authorities by seeking to register to vote en masse. In this interview, San Francisco journalist Ralph Gleason explored Gregory's motives and the implications for his entertainment career.

GLEASON: Dick, why did you go to Birmingham?

GREGORY: I guess for the same reason I went to Greenwood, Mississippi.

GLEASON: Okay, why did you go to Mississippi?

GREGORY: Well, as I read the account of what was going on in these areas in the South, and thought of the three kids I have, and knowing that the people that are breaking down the barriers down South are not only breaking them down for themselves, but for myself, my wife, and my family, I feel that it's part of my job to help them break it down, being that all of us will reap the benefits from this. I debated the night before I flew into Greenwood, Mississippi, simply because I had a new son, and I hadn't been able to get back to Chicago to see the boy. Mississippi won out because when I laid there and thought that if America had to go to war in the morning, I would be willing to go. And when I can go to any of the four corners of the world, take a chance on losing my life being away from my loved ones to guarantee a foreigner a better way of life, I must be able to go and guarantee the Negro a better way of life.

GLEASON: Was there any pressure upon you as a performer not to do this?

GREGORY: No. No one knew I was going but a couple close friends of mine. My managers found out after I got there. They wouldn't have said anything anyway because we have a relationship where they know they work for me. My agent works for me, my managers work for me, and everyone on my staff including my lawyers on down works for me. I make the decisions and the policies for Dick Gregory Enterprises.

GLEASON: Do you see this move as a role for you as a performer, as an artist, or as a human being?

GREGORY: Me as a human being. I've said many times I'm an individual first, an American second, and a Black man third, but I'm Black before I'm an entertainer, so my decision to go into any area or to participate in any affair is as an individual. I have never allowed restrictions in my contracts with club owners that if I'm in town, and there's a benefit that I feel is for a worthy cause, I don't have to clear it with the owners. I try to stay away from [events] where there's nothing but entertainment, but other than that, these restrictions where you can't come into the area sixty days before and after, I never honor these at all.

GLEASON: But inevitably your public personality as a performer gets involved in this, doesn't it?

GREGORY: Not with me.

GLEASON: Does it get involved with the people that you work for at clubs, or with the audience?

GREGORY: No, I have never found that, maybe mainly because I don't look for it. But I have never found it to be so.

GLEASON: When you got to Mississippi, were they aware of you as a performer? Were you just another individual?

GREGORY: No. I could have gone to any area of the South with less impact because in many areas of the South, Dick Gregory was unheard of. You take the Delta area. The average Negro's take-home pay is $300 a year. He's not reading the type of books that I've been getting write-ups in for the last two years. Television—90 percent of them do not have them. So when I flew the planeload of surplus food into the Delta, this is what made Dick Gregory in this area. The police knew this. This is why I never got arrested in Greenwood, Mississippi, because a lot of the Negroes thought I was a preacher. Many never knew I was an entertainer.

GLEASON: The cops all knew, though?

GREGORY: Oh yes, the cops knew. When I decided to go into Greenwood, I never realized the impact it would have on the American press. I never knew the amount of FBI agents that would be coming down. I called a fellow by the name of Aaron Henry in Clarksdale, Mississippi, when I airlifted the food in. I didn't have too much time because I had to go right back to the Playboy Club in Chicago. But I told Aaron the first time I had a couple of days off, I would be back. I had a Monday and Tuesday off, and I was going down to speak—Monday night in Greenwood, Tuesday in Clarksdale. It was only after I got in this area that I really got to see firsthand what was going on because when I brought the food in, I didn't get to see. We unloaded it and I got in a car, and I went right back to Memphis and jetted out. Not until I got there to speak that night, and watched and listened.

I was briefed on a couple things. For instance, in Greenwood, the population is 22,000 white, 24,000 Negro. There's one hospital in the whole town, with 168 beds, and 130 were for whites. Well, a Negro can't even afford to get sick there. There's not one Negro doctor. So when these people decide to march down to this court building, and sign their names and identify themselves, they're also saying that I'm giving up all my medical care because these doctors will not see them anymore. When a person says, "I'll do this for freedom," this opens your eyes.

GLEASON: How many of them vote, of the 24,000?

GREGORY: We never could find out because you go in and you register to vote, and it's about a month before they let you know how many have actually passed the test. From looking at the tests, if they decided no one would pass the test, no one would pass. Out of the five pages, there are only actually two questions. One is to write in such-and-such article of the Mississippi Constitution. The second question is the one that throws you. They say, "In the space below, explain what your interpretation of this means." Even if you have the exact interpretation of it, when the clerk grades the paper, [they say] this is not right. This is the problem that they have. So, it mainly ended up being a demonstration of, for the first time in a hundred years, being able to walk down to the court building in a large group. On the day the police were real worried we had about fifty people down to register, they followed us, didn't want us to walk in large lines, so I asked the police commissioner, "Wouldn't it be wild if you found out all they were really trying to do is pay their water tax?"

GLEASON: When you said things like that to people like [the commissioner], what was their reaction?

GREGORY: Oh, well this Hammond, this is probably one of the most beautiful individuals I ever met in my life. On the outside he's for the people there, but on the inside he has enough sense to know what's going on. And anyone that would call the Greenwood jail for me—I wasn't there, even though a lot of people felt I was arrested—he would send a cop out to bring me the message. This boiled down to seeing who could outwit who.

GLEASON: How does this affect you as a professional performer? It would seem to me that a nightclub owner that's going to hire you says to himself, "Well, I hire Dick Gregory. How do I know he's not going to split?"

GREGORY: Well, he has no guarantee. No more guarantee than you'd have signing me on a contract during World War III. You never know when I'm going to be drafted. Same difference.

GLEASON: Do you see this as World War III?

GREGORY: This is the most vicious war ever known in the history of man. Because you have one side with all the guns, all the police, all the dogs, and the law on their side. And the other side has no ammunition, no guns, and will not fight. But they are willing to die against these soldiers for the right to vote, the right to dignity, and the right to say, "I will be counted as a man."

GLEASON: Can you use this experience of yours in your work professionally?

GREGORY: No. I think all the great writers have found out: when you commercialize, you have to water down the truth.

SPEECH AT ST. JOHN'S BAPTIST CHURCH, BIRMINGHAM

(May 10, 1963)

At the behest of Martin Luther King Jr., on May 6, 1963, Dick Greg-
ory joined the last week of civil rights demonstrations in Birmingham,
Alabama, directed by the Southern Christian Leadership Conference
(SCLC). He was promptly arrested with hundreds of other protesters
and spent four days in the Birmingham Jail. At the end of the decisive
week, he spoke at the final, triumphant mass meeting in Birmingham.

I'll tell you one thing: it sure is nice being out of that prison over
there. A lot of people asked me when I went back to Chicago last
night, they said, "Well, how are the Negroes in Birmingham taking
it? What did they act like? What did they look like?" I said, "Man,
I got off a plane at ten thirty, arrived at the motel at eleven, and by
one o'clock I was in jail." So I know what you all mean when you
refer to the good old days. I asked one guy, "What is the 'good old
days'?" and he said, "10 BC and 15 BC." And I said, "You're not
that old," and he said, "Nah, I mean ten, fifteen years before Bull
Connor got here."

Man, they had so many Negroes in jail over there, the day I was there, when you looked out the window and see one of them walking around free, you knew he was a tourist. I got back to Chicago last night and a guy said, "Well, how would you describe the prison scene?" and I said, "Baby, just wall-to-wall us."

So, I don't know, really, when you stop to think about it. That was some mighty horrible food they were giving us over there. First couple of days, it taste bad and look bad and after that it tasted like home cooking. Matter of fact, it got so good the third day that I asked one of the guards for the recipe.

Of course, you know, really, I don't mind going to jail myself. I just hate to see Martin Luther King in jail. For various reasons: one, when the final day get here, he is going to have a hard time trying to explain to the boss upstairs how he spent more time in jail than he did in the pulpit. When I read in the paper in Chicago that they had him in jail on Good Friday, I said that's good. And I was praying and hoping when they put him in Good Friday, they had checked back there Easter Sunday morning and he would have been gone. That would have shook up a lot of people, wouldn't it?

I don't know how much faith you have in newspapers, but I read an article in the paper a couple days ago, where the Russians—did you see this, they gave it a lot of space—the Russians claim they found Hitler's head. Well, I want to tell you that's not true. You want to find Hitler's head, just look right up above Bull Connor's shoulders. To be honest with you, I don't know why you call him Bull Connor. Just say "Bull." That's half of it.

I don't know, when you stop and think about it, I guess little by little when you look around, it kind of looks like we're doing all right. I read in the paper not too long ago, they picked the first Negro astronaut. That shows you so much pressure is being put on

Washington, these cats just reach back and they trying to pacify us real quickly. A lot of people were happy that they had the first Negro astronaut; well, I'll be honest with you, not myself. I was kind of hoping we'd get a Negro airline pilot first. They didn't give us a Negro airline pilot; they gave us a Negro astronaut. You realize that we can jump from back of the bus to the moon?

That's about the size of it. I don't know why this cat let them trick him into volunteering for that space job. They not even ready for a Negro astronaut. You have never heard of no dehydrated pigs' feet.

I never would have let them give me that job, myself. No, I wouldn't. That's one job I don't think I could take. Just my luck, they'd put me in one of them rockets and blast it off. We'd land on Mars somewhere. A cat would walk up to me with twenty-seven heads, fifty-nine jaws, nineteen lips, forty-seven legs, and look at me and say, "I don't want you marrying my daughter neither." Oh, I'd have to cut him.

So, I don't know, when you stop and think about it, we're all confused. I'm very confused. I'm married. My wife can't cook. No, it's not funny. How do you burn Kool-Aid? You know, raising kids today is such a difficult task. These kids are so clever. They're so hip. My son walked up to me not too long ago, he said, "Daddy, I'm going to run away from home. Call me a cab." I remember when I was a kid, I told my father the same thing. I said, "Pa, if you don't give me a nickel, I'm leaving home." He said, "Son, I'm not gonna give you one penny, and take your brothers with you." I remember when I was a kid, if my parents wanted to punish me, it was simple. They told me, "Get upstairs to your room," which was a heck of a punishment because there was no upstairs.

And I just found out something not too long ago I didn't know.

You don't walk into a kid's room anymore. You have to knock first. My daughter told me, "I'm three years old. I've got rights." What do you mean, you have rights? You haven't even got a job. I said, "Honey, you don't know how fortunate you are: you have a room by yourself, a bed by yourself." I said, "Honey, do you realize when I was three years old, so many of us slept in the same bed together, if I went to the washroom in the middle of the night, I had to leave a bookmark so I wouldn't lose my spot." She said, "Daddy, aren't you happy you're living with us now?"

Let me tell you about this daughter of mine. Last Christmas Eve night, I walked into my daughter's room. I said, "Michele, tonight's Christmas Eve, it's 11:30, you're three years old. Go to bed and get ready for Santa Claus." She said, "I don't believe in Santa Claus." I said, "What in the world you mean you don't believe in Santa Claus, and I'm picking up the tab?" She said, "Daddy, I don't care what you picking up. I don't believe in Santa Claus." I said, "Why?" She said, "Because you know darn good and well there ain't no white man coming into our neighborhood after midnight." So, you see, we have problems.

I'd like to say, it's been a pleasure being here. A lot of people wonder, why would I make a decision to go to Greenwood, Mississippi? Why would I make a decision to come to Birmingham? When I lay in my bed at night and I think if America had to go to war tonight, I would be willing to go to any of the four corners of the world; and if I am willing to go and lay on some cold dirt, away from my loved ones and my friends and take a chance on losing my life to guarantee some foreigner that I've never met equal rights and dignity, I must be able to come down here.

You know it is such a funny thing how the American mind works, and this is white and Negro alike. How many on both sides of the fence say, "Well, did he go down for publicity?" One, I don't need publicity. But the amazing thing is if I had decided to quit show business and join the Peace Corps and go to South Vietnam, nobody would have said anything about publicity. Only when you decide to help us, you get a complaint.

You people here in the South are the most beautiful people alive in the world today. The only person in this number one country in the world that knows where he's going and have a purpose is the southern Negro—bar none. When you break through and get your freedom and your dignity, then we up north will also break through and get our freedom and our dignity. Because up north we have always been able to use the South as our garbage can. But when you make these white folks put that lid on this garbage can down here, we are going to have to throw our garbage in our own backyard, and it's going to stink worse than it stinks down here.

One of the greatest problems the Negro has in America today is that we have never been able to control our image. The man downtown has always controlled our image. He has always told us how we're supposed to act. He has always told us a nigger knows his place—and he doesn't mean this, because if we knew our place, he wouldn't have to put all those signs up. And if you think we know our place, let one of us get $2 uptight on our rent and 50 cents in our pocket and we'll kick the hinges off them doors downtown to open up.

But we have never been able to control our image. He's always told us about a Negro crime rate, to the extent that you have finally decided to believe it. This is the bad part about not being able to control your image. I've always said, "What Negro crime rate?" Look at it. We not raping three-year-old kids. We haven't put forty sticks of dynamite in Mother's luggage and blew one of them airplanes out the sky. And I don't care what they say about us, we've never lynched anybody. So what Negro crime rate? If you want to see a true Negro crime rate, watch television. Look at all them gangster movies; you never see us. Of course now, you can look at TV week in and week out and look at all those doctor series they have on television and you'd be led to believe a Negro never gets sick.

For some reason, not being able to control our image has made us almost ashamed of us. Because anything he decides to tell us, about us, we believe it, and become ashamed of it. Negro crime rate? Sure, a lot of us get arrested. Why? The answer is right out there in the street, every day. You got a southerner out there in the police department that is probably the lowest form of man walking the Earth today. Now here's a man out there, didn't like you in the first place. Now he's got a gun. What is your crime rate supposed to look like?

They have gotten to the point where they've made you ashamed of relief. "Don't talk to so-and-so. She's on ADC [Aid for Dependent Children]." I was on relief twenty years, back home. It wasn't funny, but I wasn't ashamed of it because had they given my daddy the type of job he deserved to have, we wouldn't have needed no relief. And the day this white man—not only in the South, but in America—gives us fair housing, fair jobs, equal schools, and the other things the Constitution says we're supposed to have, we will relieve him of relief. Until that day rolls around, let him pay his dues. The check ain't much, but it's steady.

And then you read a lot and hear a lot about Negro women with illegitimate kids. Oh, this really makes you ashamed. Each time you pick up one of them newspapers, one of them magazines, reading about Negro women with illegitimate kids, check the article out and see who wrote it. Some chick living in a neighborhood where they've got abortion credit cards.

Never been able to control our image, all at once we're ashamed. Talked about us for so long, we started believing it. Talked about our hair for so long, for a hundred years now we've been trying to straighten our wig out. Wouldn't it be wild if you find out one day that we had natural hair and there was something wrong with theirs?

Every time you look around, they're talking about a Negro with a switchblade to the extent we don't want to carry switchblades no more. Well, I keep me a switchblade. I got a deal going with the white folks. I don't say nothing about their missiles, and they don't say nothing about my switchblade. Here's a man who owns half the missiles in the world and want to talk about my switchblade. I don't know one Negro in America that manufactures switchblades. Now he going to sell me some and then talk about it after I get it.

He made a lot of mistakes, and had all you older people been able to figure out the mistakes he made like the younger people figured them out, we would have had this a long time ago. Yep, he made a lot of mistakes. Here's a man that got over here and didn't even know how to work segregation. Didn't even know how prejudice worked. He just wanted to try it. He said, "We got a bunch of them niggers, let's try it," and he messed up. 'Cause any clown knows that if you want to segregate somebody and keep them down forever, you put them up front. They made the great mistake of putting us in the back; we've been watching them for three hundred years. Yeah, that was a big mistake they made. We know how dirty they get their underwear because we wash them for them. They don't even know if we wear them or not.

They made a couple of mistakes. It is beginning to catch up with them now. One of the biggest mistakes they made is that white lady. All at once they think all we want is a white lady. And they don't understand why we want one. It's their fault. Aspirin can't advertise aspirin without one of them white ladies, and so we feel we need a white lady to get rid of our headache. Every year General Motors advertises those Cadillacs with those blondes and know we gonna get one of them cars. Every time I go to the movie, I can't see none of them pretty little chocolate drops in them dynamite love scenes; they show me one of them white ladies. Every time I look at Miss America, I can't see no Mau Mau queens; they show me one of them white ladies. So what am I supposed to watch? But I'll make a deal with the good white brother, yes, if he let me turn on television and see some of my women advertising some of them products we use so much of, if he let me go to the movie and see some of my folks in some of them good scenes, and if he let me turn on television this year and see seven of us on Miss America to make up, then anytime he see me with a white woman I'll be holding her for the police.

Again, I'd like to say it is completely and totally my pleasure being here. I don't know how many of you in the house have kids that were in jail. Four days I was in jail. Had you been there, as I was, walking through, listening, it was really something to be proud of, really something to be proud of. And if something ever happens and you have to do it again, don't hesitate. Because the only thing we have left now that's gonna save this whole country, and eventually the world, is us. He taught us honesty, and he forgot how it worked himself. Nothing wrong with that white man downtown. We just have to teach him how to act. He doesn't know how to be fair. He doesn't know we'd never complain if he was fair. "Keep me a second-class citizen, but just don't make me pay first-class taxes.

Send me to the worst schools in America, if you must, but when I go downtown to apply for that job, don't give me the same test you give that white boy." Now we are going to have to teach him how to be fair, and the only thing we have to do it with is ourselves.

This is it. This is all we have. He has all the police, all the dogs; never thought I'd see the day the fireman would turn water on us in summertime and make us hotter, but they did. What these white folks don't realize is a terrific amount of police brutality that I have witnessed down here. What they fail to realize is when you let a man bend the law and aim it at us, he'll aim that same law at you.

These are the problems that we have. Again, I am as far away from you as Delta Airline is; anytime there is any problem, I will be back. Thank you very much and God bless you.

MEDGAR

On June 12, 1963, civil rights activist Medgar Evers was fatally shot in the back outside his home in Jackson, Mississippi. The following is an excerpt of a recording Dick Gregory did with Robert Lipsyte for his autobiography soon after Evers's assassination.

America had lost a great man. Here's a man who would go anywhere there was trouble in the whole state of Mississippi. Go with a smile. Never had a day of hate on his face. Medgar Evers. Shot in the back!

Then again, I guess, what difference does it make where a man shoots you. Laying in the bushes, shot him in the back.

I rushed back to the apartment where I was staying in San Francisco, called Medgar Evers's home, and a party answered the phone. I confirmed it. Yes, Medgar Evers was dead. A guy I just finished talking to two days ago. A guy that a week and a few days before had called me to inform me that my son, Dick Jr., was dead. And that same telephone at his house that he used to call me, now someone's on that same phone telling me, yes, Medgar was killed.

I sat up all that night thinking about Medgar. Knowing at that time that maybe it will be a long time before America finds out what a great man we lost. Releasing those pictures with nobody but white folks bleeding has to come to something else.

I called all over the country that night. Everyone was upset. Called different taverns all over the country to find out what was going on, find out the tempo. White papers handled it nice. A lot of Blacks wouldn't get too mad because a lot of them were embarrassed because they never heard of Medgar Evers. And the white press all over the world was talking about Medgar Evers. I guess we were happy that a great man was being exposed, not only to white America, but to many Blacks who never heard of him.

I was out in California. Now they reached back and pulled out tapes of a speech Medgar had made. When he made it, they used maybe two minutes of it. Now they're running the whole hour. Funny about a great man, when he dies, if the whole world didn't know him, they can learn about him and decide for themselves. They decided that we had lost a great man in this country.

The lines stretched for miles, four, five, ten abreast, walking behind Medgar Evers. The line stretched so far behind it looked like a bunch of ants: old folks, young folks, Black folks, white folks, raggedy folks, dressed-up folks, southerners, northerners, nappy hair, pressed hair. Stacy Adams, Edwin Clapp, Johnston & Murphy, Thom McAn, Buster Brown, barefooted.

Yep. They walked and they walked. Got to look at this picture over here to see what it looked like. Boy, oh, it looked like we had enough folks to march on God that day.

We turned the corner. Very amazing. Life is funny. The same white police that were fighting Medgar Evers so hard were the same white police that were directing traffic. The same white people that lived in a town and didn't open up their mouths when a man was fighting for right and truth and justice and let him get killed. These same white folks—and this same white cop was stopping them and saying, "I'm sorry, buddy, but you got to wait." Yep, we killed him; now we got to wait.

I guess every white man that gets ready to kill a man or any man in the world that gets ready to kill a good man who's fighting for right should give him a picture of that funeral procession, because you find out when you shoot right down to the ground, more right rises up.

SELMA SPEECHES

(October 1963)

As in many places in Mississippi, Black citizens were the majority in Dallas County, Alabama, but just 1 percent of them were registered to vote. As they had in Greenwood, SNCC conducted demonstrations and planned a march in Selma, Alabama, on October 7 to empower Black residents to attempt to register together on what they called Freedom Day. In Dick Gregory's absence, his wife Lillian was jailed for nearly two weeks during the Selma demonstrations while four months pregnant with twins. Dick later arrived and spoke at two mass meetings to encourage fearful Black residents.

SPEECH AT BROWN CHAPEL AME CHURCH, SELMA (OCTOBER 4, 1963)

Thank you very much. I can't tell you what a pleasure it is being here. I'm just sorry I had to show up ten days late. But I think I was able to see my all-time first: to see a white southern dumb cop writing. I've never been able to see one writing, but he's writing tonight. Every time I've seen them in the meetings, they've always had tape recorders, but this one must have a little piece of education he got from somewhere. That's the first one I've known to have enough intelligence to write, and I still don't believe he's got anything on that paper. Then again, I think we'd better not put him down too much or laugh at him too hard because during one of those good songs I caught him kind of shaking his finger there a little bit. That's wonderful when a man comes to spy on us and ends up shaking with us for a few minutes. That means he can be saved too.

Yeah, that's a great thing. It always amazed me to wonder how southern white folks will knock themselves out, pose as all kind of everything, but a cop to slip in a Negro meeting—and we haven't gotten around to wanting to slip into a Ku Klux Klan rally. So, I think it speaks for itself. The whole world wants to slip in and be around right and good and godliness, but only fools want to be around filth.

Because it just knocks me out to see white folks talk about how much they dislike us, how they can't get along with us. And I'm glad they was in here tonight to witness two Negro women that one of them—and I don't even have to put them together—any one of them probably have more education and more intelligence than this whole police department put together.

Now these are the people that don't want to be around us. These are the people that complain twenty-four hours a day. These are the peons; these are the idiots that do the dirty work. These are the dogs that get paid to do all the biting. These are the ones that have become big men among small people. These are the ones that need something like that, and many southern white men need the job of being a southern cop. When you sit down, put yourself in a southern white man's shoes. Think about it for a minute. Just think about it for a minute. A southern white man. The only thing you have to identify with is a drinking fountain, a toilet, and the right to be able to call me "nigger." And before we really put him down, put yourself in his shoes. Think. That's all you have to identify with in the world is a toilet. Then you know why they got toilet ways.

Put yourself in this southern white man's shoes and you'll understand why he would blow up one of your churches. You'll understand why he will fight you the way he will fight you. Everyone was so upset over a white man dynamiting a church. And you forgot John Grant put forty sticks of dynamite in his white mammy's luggage and blew her plane out of the sky.

Put yourself in this southern white man's shoes for just a few minutes and you'll almost get out there and want to hit your own self in the head with a stick. Put yourself in this southern white man's shoes. Just think. He never owned anything new, ignorant, can't read, can't write. But when he wants to feel superior to you, he can walk into his own toilet. That's the difference. And when he loses that toilet and we plug up one of those fountains and when he calls us nigger, we fix it in a way he has to say it a little bit pretty; he's lost it all. He will have lost it all.

This is a heck of a thing to be a white man in America and when you're threatened about losing your toilet, you're ready to kill. This is a heck of a thing to be a white man in America and when you find out you can't call me nigger no more, not like you used to call me nigger, because he's almost about to find out who that nigger really is. He's almost about to find out. Every white man in America knows we are Americans. They know we are Negroes, and many of them know us by our name. And when he calls us a nigger, he's calling us something that we're not, so it must exist in his mind. So if nigger exists in his mind, who is the nigger?

Now let's take it a step further. Let's take it one step further. We know this is a Bible. We know this is a book. Now when I sit here and call this a bicycle, I have called this something that it is not. The bicycle must exist where? In my mind! I'm the sick one, right? So that's why we really don't have to worry about these folks. We don't have to get mad when a white man calls us boy. He knows how old we are. That means he's got doubts about his own manhood.

If you think white folks in this country hate us, they need us. You think these redneck crackers down here hate us? I just wish it was some kind of way. I just wish it was some kind of way that we would lay down and go to sleep tomorrow night and when they wake up through the grace of God, we would all be gone. They would go crazy looking for us. "Where are they? Please y'all, come back."

If they could wake up and every Negro in America would be, like, gone. Oh, I would give a million dollars to just slip back and watch *The Huntley-Brinkley Report*. I can just see it now. "There are no clues as to where the Negroes are." Oh, the news would be wild that day. "Ku Klux Klan have announced due to all the Negroes gone in America, they are moving to Alaska and now are going to lynch the Eskimos."

Oh, can't you just hear the news? "Governor Wallace decided that due to the fact that all the Negroes are gone and he has nothing else to campaign for, he's still going to stay in politics and campaign against keeping Jews out of pizza joints." Yeah, we could just wake up one day and all of us would be gone. Oh, it would be some wild news that night. I can just see the headlines back north: "Seven Chitlin Manufacturers Found Out the Negroes Were Gone and Committed Suicide."

Yes, if we could only leave here for three days. Three days. Just leave them down here by themselves so they can find out who the nigger is. That would be all we would need. But it looks like we're going to have to do it the hard way and stay here and educate these folks.

And we're going to educate them. We're going to teach them how to live and teach them how to act. And when you hear all this talk that we don't know how to live and we don't know how to act and when the Negro can act like him, he'll accept us. I'd rather be accepted by an elephant first if I had to act like that.

To be accepted. Here's a man here. Thank God this white man has always had a conscience, but he's always wondering what's wrong with the Negro. People say, well they've had slaves before. No slave in the history of the world had to go through what the American Negro slave had to go through because we had a master that was lower than us. Never in the history of slavery did you have a white man go out in the barn and have a sex affair with all the slaves like this dog did.

Oh, you always had masters that would go out every so often and pick the Liz Taylor out of the group, but the slaves were proud. We had a master that we couldn't even respect. We had a master that was so much below us and knew it, he said, "Sure, let them ride on the same bus. Just put them in the back." No master in the history of slavery has ever wanted to be with his slaves, front or back. But we had a man who was so low down and so ignorant, he didn't even qualify to have slavery, because if he qualified, he would have set it up right. He set it up wrong.

The biggest fool in the world knows if you want to segregate me and put me down, you don't put me in the back where I can watch you for two hundred years. The biggest fool in the world knows if you want to keep me down you don't keep me under conditions where I can become stronger than you. And this is his greatest mistake, whether he knows it or not. He does not represent strength.

He represents a gun. He represents crooked ways. He represents dirty, trampy dealings. That's why we can let him in here because we're stronger than he is, and if you don't believe it, watch a demonstration. When they round up a bunch of Negroes and all they have to say is, "You're under arrest," and pull the wagon up and they'll walk into the car, watch what happens. Watch what happens. A little baby could arrest Negro demonstrators because we intend to go to jail. So it's no big thing when they do it.

It's no big thing at all because the man says, "You're under arrest," we're going, "I don't know who they're trying to impress." Those little white kids at home who are still young enough to believe that they're somebody, or what? But there hasn't been one demonstration in America this year that called for a Negro to be knocked down because when we go out, we intend to go to jail.

Oh, when a man slips so low he forgets about God. The dirtiest hoodlums that ever lived and you're looking at it now, on television. They got this chump up in Washington, DC, on a Senate investigation. These people have talked about all types of murders, all types of everything, and as I sit every day and look at this hoodlum testify, the hundreds of thousands of millions of dollars and the amount of dope they slipped in, I can't help but feel kind of happy for them and feel sorry for these fools like this who would throw tear gas in a church. The dirtiest hoodlums in the world still haven't lost respect for God's church, Black or white. Here's a man who will become so bitter and so insane on the hate appeal, if it means losing God to keep this thing away from him, he'd do it.

And you know why he would do it? Because he has had a little bit of God in him. He had a conscience and he had to tell himself for a long time that you were inferior to him. He knew better, but he had to keep telling himself that because God gave him a little piece of conscience in order for him to rest at night. He had to convince himself beyond a shadow of a doubt that he was better than you and it ran him crazy. Living a lie for one hundred years and you would throw dynamite in a church. Living hate for one hundred years and you would tear-gas this same crowd. This man had to sleep, and he had this thing. That he was better than you. And he said that, and he'd wake up every now and then and look around, and he still kept believing. And he sets up little hurdles, little roadblocks in front of you so he can still tell his warped mind that he must tell himself this and he must believe this because he has to leave here tonight and go back to a shack. That cop on the street has got to knock you down and hope he can whop you for five hours because he's got to go home to something that's less than what you have to go home to.

Because the truth is in your house. This is a man that's human. We fought wars with him, we helped him plant his crop, and we raised his kids, that's right, and he went so stone crazy he's tear-gassing ours.

But we raised his kids. And that Black woman never told him that she raised that white boy of his that lynched her Black son. She never told him that. She said, "The Lord's going to take care of him." Well, that's right. That's the Lord out there in that street. That's the Lord that's going to be out there Monday going down to register to vote. He's going to take care of him.

See, we don't have to be violent. We have the three most violent things a man could ever use on our side. We have truth, we have justice, and we have the United States Constitution. With those three things, you can't lose. You can't lose with those three things. This chump might kill you wrongly, but he'll never win because he hasn't got the truth on his side. And if you don't think those three things on your side create a winner, think again.

If the South today wanted to raise the educational standards of the dumb southern white boy, it would be a simple matter. But he does not have the intelligence to know so we have to tell him. If he wanted to raise the educational standards of his son, you know what he would do? He would pull the Negro teachers out of the Negro schools and put them in the white schools and take the white teachers and put them in the Negro schools. And his boy would learn something.

I know I don't have to break it down for you, but I don't trust his intelligence so just give me a few minutes. All I'm really trying to say is that I want to prove to him beyond a shadow of a doubt that 90 percent of the southern Negro teachers are much better equipped and better qualified than the white teachers. . . . I don't want to disturb him now because we've got him concentrating. The reason that the Negro teacher in the South would be better qualified and better equipped to teach his dumb son is simple: We were denied the pleasure of going to a bad University of Alabama. We were denied the pleasure of going to a bad University of Mississippi, and consequently we went north to Harvard, Yale, NYU, Howard, UCLA, and the University of Chicago.

We went to the best universities in the world and then came back home. So due to the fact that we, as Negroes, were denied the privilege to go to one of those bad, low-paying white colleges, we had to go up north and go to a good school. Thank God it backfired on them again.

Through this man's dumb, stupid mistakes and hate, he has made the American Negro the strongest man in the world today. And he knows it and he doesn't know it. That's why he gets his little cattle prods and he gets all his police out. Because what he realizes is we're strong and he doesn't want to believe it. There are two basic things that go in to build up a strong man: joy and pain. Joy makes you want to live, and pain teaches you how to live.

There's not a race alive on the face of the Earth that has had as much hope as the American Negro. So that makes us the number one strong man in this country. And what makes it so beautiful is, here's a man sitting over here that although he has so much hate for me, he doesn't understand that I decide the fate and the destiny of this country today. Because the Negro in America today is the number one strong man, and you southern Negroes are stronger than all. He is going to learn this one day.

SPEECH AT FIRST BAPTIST CHURCH, SELMA (OCTOBER 5, 1963)

Thank you very much and again, good evening. I guess this is about the first time in my life that I ever requested a church song. I usually listen to all of them. Some I like and understand, and some I don't like. But I asked them to sing that song because as I sit back there and wonder, had we been living in that day and era of the crucifixion of Christ—when it was taking place, when it was going on—and had we turned and run the other way, I wonder how we would have felt twenty years later, thirty years later, knowing we weren't there and could have been there.

If I could honestly prove beyond a shadow of a doubt that I had some kinfolks in that same era and same location and they didn't show up to say no more than, "I'm with you, baby," I would be ashamed of them and ashamed of myself.

We're going through an era today equally as important. It's so amazing how we come to the church every day and cry over the crucifixion of Christ. And we don't cry over these things that are going on around and among us, when if He was here now, He would cry and take those nails again for this problem.

It just so happened that in His day and time, religion was the big problem. Today, same problem, only it's a color. What do you think would happen to Christ tonight if He arrived in this town, a Black man, and tried to vote Monday? What do you think would happen? Would you be there? Then how come you're not with these kids? Because He said, "Whatever happens to the least, happens to us all."

And I wonder, one day when this final push is over, when the whole world knows that this was the work of God, when they sit back in the future and sing "Were you there?" I wonder how many of us have to hang our head in shame. How many of us will have to hang our heads in shame?

Let's analyze the situation. We're not saying, "Let's go downtown and take over City Hall." We're not saying, "Let's stand on the rooftops and throw bricks at white folks." We're not saying, "Let's get some butcher knives and some guns and make them pay for what they've done." We're saying we want what you said belongs to us. You have a constitution. Me, as a Black man going to a Black school, you make me sit down and take a test on the United States Constitution. You have never made me take a test on this Bible. Mama had to give that to me at home. You have kept me in a segregated school, but you make me take a test on a constitution that hasn't worked for anyone but you. And you expect me to learn it from front to back, or you're going to flunk me. So, I learned it when I didn't even want to learn it. And I passed it.

You made me stand up as a little kid and sing "God Bless America," "America the Beautiful," and all those songs the white kids were singing. I pledged my allegiance to the flag. That's what I'm asking you for today.

No Negro had anything to do with sitting down and writing the

Constitution, so no white man can say we tricked him. He wrote that himself. And he told the whole world about it. He said it was fair. He said it was just, and he's carried your son to war to die for it.

And when you tell me a white man, with his corrupt beliefs, can come and get your boy and send him to Korea, send him to Germany, to die for something you're not going to be a part of, and a man can't get your daughter, can't get your son, can't get you to go to jail—unbelievable his system has warped our minds this much.

It's unbelievable you would let your son go and fight in a foreign country for a neighborhood he can't live in. But you won't let your kids march or demonstrate, you won't demonstrate for what's yours. This, I can't understand.

That's why I'm here. That's what really made me make up my mind. If America went to war in the morning, I'm going. Because as corrupt as the system is, I dig it. But I'm going. And then I had to stop and think. If I can subject myself to go to some foreign land, take a chance of being away from my wife, my family, my loved ones, and take a chance on losing my life to guarantee some foreigner, that's living some place I can't even spell, a better way of life than I can my own brothers and sisters, then there must be something wrong with me.

That's when I made my decision to come into the South, knowing when I stepped off the plane I could be killed. Knowing that getting involved might mean I wouldn't eat. Knowing that I might go to jail. But I tell you what. I think jail is the best place. Jail is the best place.

When a man can take a policeman who's supposed to be upholding the law and use him against you, then I think jail is the best place. We talked about bandits and villains all over the world, we know of none on record that have blown up a church.

Do you realize the incident that happened in Birmingham—the incidents that happen many places in the South—that had that same incident happened in North Korea, in West Berlin or South Vietnam, America would have been at war? Are you ready for this? You would have been upset.

Had you read about the Communists blowing up a church, you would have been upset. This one you're scared to even talk about around white folks. Ha, ha, ha. They had to tell you that Monday how sorry they were, and I daresay how many of you made like you didn't even know it had happened?

This is the problem that we have. This is the problem that we're faced with. It's in our hands now. You are the soldiers whether you wanted to be the soldiers or not. For some reason you kept saying, "Turn the other cheek." You kept praying to God every time something happened to you, and for some reason or another, He believed you. As He looked down, out of all the peoples in the world, He probably had to nudge His Daddy and say, "I've been checking them, Pa, for a hundred years. They're the ones."

"How do you know?"

"Well, look what they been going through. Just look at the books. Look at the lynchings. They haven't fought back. Look at the shootings. They haven't fought back. Look at the bad things, Poppa, they've gone through."

"Yeah, Son. It kind of reminds Me of Your story."

In 1963 He probably nodded His head and gave you the ball. Now the best thing for us to do is to get ourselves together and take it or give it back to Him. Take it or give it back to Him.

I can't believe a parent would worry about a kid being in jail overnight, and then again, I can believe, I guess. But how can you worry about a kid being in jail overnight and live with him under the system you had to bring him up in?

I can understand a white man worrying about his kid being in jail, because he's missing something. For fifty years they've been telling us about a Negro crime rate. Telling us we do all the crime. Never came to your house once and said, "Miss So and So, would you talk to your kids and keep them out of jail?" Now all at once they want to talk to you in the middle of the night. Why? Because there's something that happens to a white man when he has to look at a Black man in jail for right.

There's something that happens to a man's conscience when he has to look at your kids at night. But nothing seems to happen to this man when he looks at the horrible things that happen to your kids growing up. Because it happens so subtly and we have accepted it so nicely, he really can't see it. And the bad part about it is we really can't see it either.

When was the last time you felt your ears growing? But they grow. When was the last time you could feel your little feet growing into big feet? But they grow. When was the last time you felt your hair growing? But it grows.

And as these things happen to us, their problem slips up on us. It slips up on us in a way you can't tell, or in a way you don't want to tell, because every man knows when he needs a haircut. Every man knows when his feet are too big. But in a one-hundred-year period, we seem not to know what this problem is doing to us because we have accepted it. Did we accept it because we wanted to do something about it? Or did we accept it because we felt this was all we could do?

We have everything to work with. It's a difficult thing when a man says, "Make me some biscuits, Mama," and he didn't bring anything home for you to make biscuits with. It's a heck of a thing. But when he has everything there and the biscuits aren't done, maybe he'll look elsewhere. Or maybe he'll give up completely.

There's a funny thing that happened in 1963, and the sooner we wake up and realize it, the better off this whole world is going to be. Because for some reason, God has put in your hands the salvation of not just America; this thing is bigger than this—the salvation of the whole world. And if you don't believe it, check the papers. Check the records.

Khrushchev and Kennedy never sat down and made a deal until you people in the South started rising up. The monks in Vietnam never started striking back for religious freedom until we had a Greenwood and a Birmingham. People are looking at you all over the world because they come over here, they see the situation here, and they gave you up. Gave you up and they couldn't understand it. The Negroes in America have the highest standard of living, the highest educational standard, the best medical care of any Black man the world over, and most whites. And we have backward countries that are getting more respect from this white man than you could ever command. That's because we grinned when he wanted us to grin. We cried when he wants us to cry. We've spent money when he wants us to spend money, and we've done without when he said, "Do without." He owns all the missiles in the whole world, then he talks about you owning a switchblade and you get ashamed of it. He started all the wars, and he talks about you cutting somebody. He doesn't give us anything else to do. He doesn't occupy my time.

He makes me feel small. He calls me everything on the job but my name, so I'm aggravated before I get home. Then he tells me about my education. He tells me about my education. Well, if it took his style of education to produce a clown that would throw some dynamite in a church, I hope we never get that.

If it took education to produce an American white man what would neatly lay forty sticks of dynamite in his mother's luggage and blow a jet plane out of the sky for some insurance money, I hope we never get that.

He could get the greatest education in the world from us if he only looked back. We could teach him the most important thing in the world today. We could teach him how to live.

I have a paper and I wish I had brought it with me tonight. I have a paper that I keep with me because it embarrasses me so many times, so many times. I have a paper from 1848, a New Orleans morning paper. And if you turn to the back you'll see where white folks were running ads offering rewards to get their runaway slaves back. Can you believe that? Nor can you believe that a white man would run an ad to get his slave back, but can you believe in 1847 we were running away, rebelling, and didn't have any plan to run to? 1848 slaves were running away.

Can you imagine what this old Negro had to go through? Can you just literally imagine a parent, a Negro woman come to a Negro man saying, "Honey, I'm pregnant," and the both of them fall on their knees and hope the baby is born deformed? Hope the baby is born crippled, with one leg. Can you imagine this is what a Negro had to go through, because if the baby was born that way he would have less chance of being a slave and more chance of having freedom?

Think about it. Think about the woman you love coming to you and saying she's pregnant with your baby and you cross your fingers and hope that baby is born crippled. Because you know if he's born healthy and strong, they'll make him a slave.

Can you imagine what it must have felt like to get on your knees and pray to your God and ask Him, "Please let it be crippled?"

This is what the slaves went through. A man would pray that his own son would have one arm, so maybe he could get some freedom. And a hundred years from there we have parallels. They worry about their kids being in jail overnight. Many parents that didn't even know where their kids were, for the first time they know where they are twenty-four hours a day. Twenty-four hours a day. And they are there for a good cause and a good reason.

How can a parent let a son play football when all he can do is help his team win a victory today that's going to be forgotten tomorrow? But you can't let your son fight for freedom—something that the whole world will profit from.

Sometimes I wonder how much this system has corrupted us. Sometimes I wonder when we will be able to see that the day is over now when we can say we're not involved. Those four kids who were killed in that church were not demonstrating in Birmingham. You don't have to participate. Just be Black. Or be white for our cause. When that bomb was thrown, somebody is going to have to be killed. We know this. Fifty percent of the killings are our fault because we let this man get crazy on us. Instead of bringing him around when we should have brought him around, we scratched our head five years too long.

FREEDOM SUMMER: INTERVIEW WITH *RAMPARTS* MAGAZINE

(June 1964)

In an effort to fully expose the nation to the brutality of white racism in Mississippi following the June 1964 murder of civil rights workers James Chaney, Michael Schwerner, and Andrew Goodman, Ramparts magazine published a special issue titled "Mississippi Eyewitness." It included an interview with Dick Gregory, who discussed his efforts to bring the killers to justice.

INTERVIEWER: Mr. Gregory, where were you when you first received news of the disappearance of the three civil rights workers?

GREGORY: I was in Moscow, Russia.

INTERVIEWER: What were you doing in Moscow?

GREGORY: I had been traveling through Europe with forty Japanese on a Ban-the-Bomb Mission, and I had been in Russia for two days. We were setting up a conference with the Russian Peace Mission there, and when I heard the news—

INTERVIEWER: How did you hear the news?

GREGORY: Through a UPI reporter in Moscow.

INTERVIEWER: And what did you do after you heard the report?

GREGORY: I rushed to the airport and got on a jet, flew to London. I left Moscow at 8:30 a.m. and got to London at 10:30, got to New York at 1:00, and Chicago at 3:00, and was in Jackson, Mississippi, that night.

INTERVIEWER: Who was your prime contact once you hit Mississippi?

GREGORY: I went to the COFO [Council of Federated Organizations] office in Jackson. From there we drove to Meridian, where Jim Farmer, the head of CORE [Congress of Racial Equality], had already arrived.

INTERVIEWER: What day did you arrive in Jackson, Mississippi?

GREGORY: Tuesday, the twenty-third of June, two days after the disappearance.

INTERVIEWER: When you were traveling in that immediate area, what was the emotional climate?

GREGORY: I got to Mississippi at night. I didn't talk to anyone but the kids from COFO, and they just knew that the three were dead. I didn't really see anyone until I got into Meridian, and since Chaney was from Meridian, the climate was very high among the Negroes.

INTERVIEWER: Were the Negroes at that time just about unanimous in their opinion that the three civil rights workers had been killed?

GREGORY: Oh, yes. They knew without a shadow of a doubt that they had been killed.

INTERVIEWER: What did you do in Meridian?

GREGORY: I met with Jim Farmer, and we tried to figure out an angle.

INTERVIEWER: An angle for what?

GREGORY: To get to talk to Sheriff [Lawrence] Rainey. A search party had gone out the night before, and we realized that this was our angle. We got enough cars together, and we went out on the highway from Meridian to Philadelphia[, Mississippi]. We were followed by the cops of Meridian. We were followed on the highway by the local police of the various counties we were going through until at one point we were met by about 150 state police. They stopped our caravan.

INTERVIEWER: How big was the caravan?

GREGORY: About sixteen cars.

INTERVIEWER: What happened when those 150 police stopped you?

GREGORY: I went up front of the caravan where they were telling us that they were having an investigation and that we could not search, which was good because now we had a stick to make a deal with. They agreed to let some of us talk to the sheriff and the deputy sheriff if we agreed to keep the kids out in the cars until we got back. We agreed to that. So they picked a few. There were about four of us who went in, and they set the meeting up. We went to the sheriff's office in Philadelphia. We walked into the sheriff's office, and they explained to us that they were very busy, that they were in the middle of an investigation, and that all they could give us was thirty minutes. Well, I thought it was kind of strange they would even see us.

INTERVIEWER: Why did you think it was strange that they would see you?

GREGORY: Because no Mississippi law enforcement agency, no law enforcement agency in the world, would see anyone not connected with the case when they are in the middle of an investigation. So the fact that they would see us meant that they were afraid of something. So we went in and sat down and—

INTERVIEWER: Excuse me, who from the sheriff's office was in this meeting?

GREGORY: That's what I'm coming to now. After about twenty minutes, they brought us into the room. I figured they were getting everything together. It was very strange; there was Rainey, [Deputy Sheriff Cecil] Price, and the chief investigator of the state highway police, another fellow I don't remember now, and the city attorney. It was very interesting. The city attorney did all the talking. He said he didn't have anything to do with it and that he wasn't mediating anything.

INTERVIEWER: This was still in the period when the three kids had only disappeared?

GREGORY: Yes. The sheriff was asked what had happened, and he said that he had arrested them because they were doing seventy-five miles an hour. I brought it to his attention that if you were doing seventy-five miles an hour, by the time you got caught, the town being so small, you'd be in another county. So then Deputy Sheriff Price said that he was the one who had arrested them.

INTERVIEWER: First Rainey said he arrested them, then Price said he arrested them?

GREGORY: Yes. They said, "You're right, they weren't going that fast. They were doing sixty-five miles an hour and it wasn't in town. It was outside of town."

INTERVIEWER: It was Rainey who said it was outside of town?

GREGORY: Yes. They looked at one another, and they looked at the city attorney. Then I noticed that for every question we asked them, the city attorney would butt in and almost explain to them how they had to answer. This was when I was aware that these men knew far more than was being said. And I smiled and I told Jim Farmer, "Let's go. We've got all we need." They got kinda shook up at the thought that we didn't use up our thirty minutes' time. On the way out, I told Farmer, "Jim, I've got the wildest idea." He said, "What?" I said, "You know, the only way we're gonna get it out is with large sums of money. If you'll put up $100,000, we'll break this case in one week." It was then I found out that CORE was broke. That's when I decided to do a thirty-day tour.

INTERVIEWER: This was a thirty-day tour to raise money for CORE?

GREGORY: Yes. I decided it was too good an idea to let go. I honestly believe that if there had been $100,000, there would have been a lot of changes in the case by now. I had to borrow some money, so I borrowed $25,000 from Hugh Hefner as a reward. I announced it that night before I left Meridian, and things started happening the next day.

INTERVIEWER: After you left the meeting, you went back to your car and then drove back to Meridian?

GREGORY: Yes. We told the sheriff we were going back to see the church that had been burned. He said he would take us by. When we said we wanted to take the whole caravan, he said that wouldn't be possible. So we decided we would just go back to Meridian. We turned all the cars around and went back to Meridian.

INTERVIEWER: It was at Meridian that you made your public statement offering the reward?

GREGORY: Yes. I had discussed it with Farmer after we left the sheriff's office. I had to make various calls. I called Joe Glaser first, and I couldn't get in touch with him. (Joe is the president of Associated Booking and also is my agent in New York.) Then I called Hugh Hefner, and he gave me the money just like that over the phone. I told him I would iron out the details when I got back into Chicago. I made the announcement that night that $25,000 was up. I knew that there were some big people involved in this, and I sincerely believe that $100,000 would have made a whole lot more people talk; $25,000 made a lot of people talk, but $100,000 would make them double-cross one another.

INTERVIEWER: So, after making your announcement in Meridian, you went back to Chicago?

GREGORY: Right.

INTERVIEWER: Have you been down there since?

GREGORY: No. We have had researchers down there. They have never left. They have stayed down there the whole time just to get information.

INTERVIEWER: As of this date, the murderers have not been arrested, nor have they been tried for the murder of the three civil rights workers. Has the FBI received all the known information about this case?

GREGORY: Oh, yes. They have all the information that's known.

INTERVIEWER: They knew that the boys had been murdered. Did any of them have any idea at that time where the bodies were?

GREGORY: No.

INTERVIEWER: How did they find the bodies?

GREGORY: I don't really know how they found them. I received a letter quite some time ago that practically pinpointed the spot where the bodies were found. I gave this letter to the FBI, and the FBI denied that the letter was any good. But they never denied the location stated in the letter. I question, with the location stated in the letter being so close to the location where they found the bodies, why it took three weeks to find the bodies and dig them up. Incidentally, they never brought the sailors back into that area to search, so I would say that they know a hell of a lot down there. It sort of looks like the FBI has been going out of its way to gather information to clear the FBI rather than to solve the crime.

INTERVIEWER: What more could the FBI do than aid in the discovery of the bodies?

GREGORY: It's not so much what more the FBI could do. It's what they have not and are not doing. You know, this whole business is crazy. If these Mississippi white Klansmen, who do not know how to plan crimes, who are ignorant, illiterate bastards, can completely baffle our FBI, what are all those brilliant Communist spies doing to us? A plane crashes and two weeks later the FBI patches up that plane so good that United can damn near use it again—and know exactly how it happened, and who did it. Do you mean to tell me that the FBI can't go into the South and make arrests for racial killings that were not planned, which were not done by clever people? Frankly, I think the FBI is lying and hiding.

INTERVIEWER: Why would the FBI be lying and hiding?

GREGORY: I think the reason is political. I don't think [J. Edgar] Hoover has much love for the Negro. When the Negro can have an uprising in New York, and without being asked, Hoover can send his FBI agents into New York, while he isn't too stuck on sending them into the South, then I have to blame Hoover, the head of the organization. I think many crimes could be solved if Hoover handled them differently. I think Hoover handles these things the way he wants to handle them. Hoover, and a lot of others, could be worried about public reaction since a law enforcement agency is involved. Americans might demand that federal troops go in, and no politician is about to send troops into any state this close to an election. A statesman would, but not a politician.

INTERVIEWER: Then you think the decision not to take strong FBI and other federal action in the Philadelphia case can be attributable somewhat to the president?

GREGORY: Yes. I think the proof is clear. About two and a half months ago, the president said that some arrests would be made soon, but there have been no arrests made yet. I don't know what LBJ calls soon, but I just figure that someone has advised him against allowing arrests to be made.

INTERVIEWER: Do you anticipate that after the election, assuming Johnson is elected, there will be some action in Philadelphia?

GREGORY: I think there will be.

INTERVIEWER: In the case of the three civil rights workers, was there at least one witness other than the killers?

GREGORY: Yes, there is one witness. One fellow who actually hid in the bushes and saw everything.

INTERVIEWER: And he was able to identify the people involved?

GREGORY: Oh, yes. He knew exactly who was doing what.

INTERVIEWER: Does the FBI have this information?

GREGORY: They have it, but I don't know if they're going to use it or not.

INTERVIEWER: Is this witness still alive?

GREGORY: Yes.

INTERVIEWER: Would you like to make a statement of your own regarding the murders of the three civil rights workers?

GREGORY: Yes. I feel that the president of the United States and the FBI are making a big mistake in playing politics with this case. They have embittered Negroes, and I would say that if mass rioting breaks out in America you could attribute a lot of it to President Johnson's handling of this case. If the murderers had been arrested, the Negro would still have faith in the government. However, nowadays when the FBI is mentioned, it is a joke to us. This is an organization that not too many months ago was held in high esteem by most Negroes. I think the president has caused great injustice to fall on America because the world has watched, and the world knows that this sort of thing would not be tolerated anywhere else in the world. We go all over the world trying to free people; we tell the South Vietnamese how to act; we tell East Germany to drop the [Berlin] Wall. Dr. Martin Luther King went to East Germany and told them to drop the wall, but we can't even get a wall dropped over here. No one else on the face of the Earth today is blowing up churches and getting away with it. We all know that if a Negro would blow up one church any place, the FBI would not sleep until they brought him in. So this proves to me that the FBI is not only a very vicious group, but also shows that the FBI, as far as the Negro is concerned, is a second Ku Klux Klan.

INTERVIEWER: What do you think would happen to the case of the three civil rights workers who were murdered and the entire civil rights movement if Senator [Barry] Goldwater were elected president?

GREGORY: I don't know what would happen to the case in Mississippi if Goldwater were elected, but the handling of it couldn't be any worse, that's for sure. As far as the civil rights movement is concerned, that's another story. You see, there comes a point in life whenever you have a thing like this revolution here—it isn't a revolution of Black against white, but a revolution of right against wrong—where nothing more can happen to hurt you. Nothing can hurt us because we have a pat hand. If Goldwater got in, Goldwater would help us because, for the first time in this country, he would bring twenty-two million Black people together. And man, to anybody who can do that I tip my hat. Goldwater would plug the loophole door in the White House where Negroes have been slipping in and out of, making deals. Once he closes that door, and no Negro can make a deal for another Negro, it's almost like plugging up a rat's hole. And any man who's had his rat's hole plugged up turns into a monster. America would have twenty-two million monsters here, plus all the good-doing white folks who would come out and commit themselves for the first time. If Martin Luther King were killed tomorrow, Negroes would come into the movement who hadn't been in the movement before. If Roy Wilkins were killed in the morning, if I were killed in the morning, Negroes would come into the movement who aren't in the movement now. So I say, why do we need Negroes killed, and good white folks killed, in order to bring Negroes into the movement when Barry Goldwater's getting into the White House would get us all in the movement? Barry Goldwater could not hurt us at all. In no shape, form, or fashion.

INTERVIEW WITH LARRY WILDE,
GREAT COMEDIANS TALK ABOUT COMEDY

While activism took up an increasing amount of his time and re-sources, in the mid-1960s Dick Gregory remained in high demand as a comedian. He had emerged as a unique voice among a path-breaking generation of postwar, topical humorists. Larry Wilde, himself an aspiring young comic, sought to document their distinc-tive perspectives through one-on-one interviews, such as this one with Gregory in 1965.

WILDE: When did you first realize you could make people laugh?

GREGORY: Oh, I've been doing that all my life.

WILDE: Even when you were young?

GREGORY: Yeah, until I went into show business, then I found out you couldn't *make* people laugh. It's like you have a baby that plays beautiful piano and you say, "Come by the house and listen to my three-year-old play the piano." That's fine, but come to Carnegie Hall and pay $5 to hear her and it's a different thing. This is when I learned how unfunny I was.

WILDE: Many comedians come from poor families and have had very unhappy childhoods. Do you think this is why they became comedians?

GREGORY: I think it has a lot to do with it. I was born and raised on relief, and I can be the world's biggest billionaire and I can tell jokes about being poor, whereas if Rockefeller's son decided to . . . he couldn't.

WILDE: Does coming from an impoverished environment enable the comedian to see things as funny?

GREGORY: No, I think the funniest humor comes from the guy in the street, who's not in show business. To be a comic is another form of being a whore. Humor is everyday life, and the funniest thing you're gonna hear is from the cab driver or the soda jerk or the guy in the factory. But there's something about the comedian that makes him able to get up and sell it . . . present it in a certain way.

WILDE: What is that?

GREGORY: I can't explain it. I don't think there's too many people who can. . . . I think the guy that would explain it wouldn't be a comedian; he'd be in the field of psychiatry or a sociologist.

WILDE: Do Blacks have a different sense of humor from the white man?

GREGORY: Oh, yes, because Black people have a different set of values from the white man. The white man lacks humor. We laugh at him; we've been laughing at him for years. Everything he seems to do we think is silly. You go to a Black movie house, and you think Blacks are loud, boisterous, ignorant, and uncouth, but they're not. . . . They're laughing at white folks. Our biggest form of entertainment has been the American white man . . . the silly things he does.

WILDE: Do people have to read the newspaper and be up on the latest news to appreciate your humor?

GREGORY: Oh, yes, definitely. They have to be well informed.

WILDE: Wouldn't that tend to limit your audience?

GREGORY: No, because you can always water it down. But I go across the country and it's amazing how tremendously the American is informed. Although sometimes not as sharply in one area as another.

WILDE: Were there any comedians you admired or patterned yourself after?

GREGORY: Yes, I'd always admired Rochester [Eddie Anderson], Amos and Andy, Redd Foxx, Slappy White. My knowledge of comedians was very limited because I didn't go to nightclubs, and before television there just wasn't that many to break through. Bob Hope had always been a favorite of mine. And Red Skelton. As you get into the game, you spread out and learn to appreciate many more, and then you find that comics are like whiskey, wine, ginger ale, bourbon, Scotch, beer—no two are the same—each one is his own brand.

WILDE: Were there specific things about the performers you like that you studied or tried to . . .

GREGORY: No, since I didn't have the money to go to nightclubs, I was never able to see too many comedians. And the few minutes you're given on TV doing an act . . . three minutes don't give you enough time to do it all.

WILDE: Now that you have the chance, what do you learn by watching other comedians?

GREGORY: I never watch them. I never have. I'm so wrapped up in them and what they're saying I could never learn anything.

WILDE: How long did it take you from the day you put together comedy material until that moment when you broke through?

GREGORY: I had steady work from '58 to '61, but I spent a lot of time figuring out what makes people laugh. If young comics only knew that when there's a little bit of hesitancy on laughing from the audience, it's because you got a streak of brilliance that's resented. Power makes people laugh. LBJ can tell unfunny jokes. Your boss can tell unfunny jokes. Power . . . there's a certain amount of surprise you get out of humor coming from power. This is why when the boss took you aside and told you an old silly-assed joke that never made any sense, you laughed.

WILDE: Is that the reason the new comic doing fresh material with a different point of view has the more difficult row to hoe?

GREGORY: You have it. Because when you come through with the mark of brilliance, you have the challenge, especially if you're not a big name. . . . You're upsetting something inside someone.

WILDE: You strike home.

GREGORY: Yeah. The audience is a very funny animal. He'll be ever so sympathetic to you when you're dying, and once you get him laughing, you have him. There's a loyalty people have to comedians. It's just unbelievable.

WILDE: If you find an audience unresponsive, do you have any tricks or gimmicks to start them laughing?

GREGORY: No, it's almost impossible for me to get an audience like that. Because I'm so strong outside the field of show business that *that's* the power itself when I walk on the stage. I can just look down and there's X amount of people that's frightened of me. I just wink and that makes them laugh. It's amazing the effect power has on people.

WILDE: When you say "power," do you mean an inner strength that you project to the audience?

GREGORY: My power lies in civil rights, and although I'm a very good comedian, I have this extra thing going for me. Consequently, I never have to worry about walking out and an audience not laughing. Sometimes I say to myself, "For ten minutes I'm going to try and not get a laugh." It's impossible. Deliver the material backwards, jump over the punch line, and you still get a laugh.

WILDE: You've been to show business what Jackie Robinson was to baseball, that is, the first Negro to break through on a national level. As the pioneer, what were some of the problems you encountered?

GREGORY: Oh, I didn't encounter that many because I was in Chicago and I never knew Negroes couldn't work in top white nightclubs, and all I was trying to do was work well enough to make $25 a night. When I broke through, I became aware of the problem of the Negro comedian working in a white nightclub. . . . Then I basically figured out most of the problems myself before I ever went to work. I knew that the white comedian . . . when the white woman got up to go pee, he's always made a comment about it, so you look for it. So when I'm onstage and see she gets up to pee, it's not only that I can't make a comment about it. The fact that I *wouldn't* make a comment still is obvious because in every other club in the history of nightclubs there's been a comment. So for me not to make a comment leaves it sticking out, you know?

WILDE: Do you think the civil rights movement also helped you progress as fast as you did?

GREGORY: Oh, yes, no doubt about it.

WILDE: A performer doing comedy is often referred to as a comedian or a comic or humorist. What do you consider yourself?

GREGORY: Comedian, social satirist, maybe a clown. The true clown knows all the social problems. When I first hit it big, people said, "You remind me of Mark Twain." That was a compliment because Mark Twain didn't pull any punches. I think the greatest social commentator of our times, and the only man I know that could equal Mark Twain, is Lenny Bruce.

WILDE: Why this great admiration for Lenny Bruce?

GREGORY: It's his brilliance. Here's a man can do three hours on any subject. I'm not talking about three silly hours—three manufactured hours. Lenny Bruce, two thousand years from now, will be one of the names that will still be remembered. He's to show business what Einstein was to science.

WILDE: Why do people laugh at you?

GREGORY: 'Cause, for one thing, I'm funny, and I use very powerful stuff, and I jam it right.

WILDE: What do you mean "jam it"?

GREGORY: I place it right where I want it to be placed and know exactly when to drop a thing. It's like a guy boxing. When you're sparring, you roll to his punch. It's the same thing with that laugh: you roll to it . . .

WILDE: When a writer submits material to you, how do you decide what's funny and what you think the audience will laugh at?

GREGORY: I never read new material until I'm in the dressing room, five minutes before I'm ready to go on. If it's funny, it'll be with me, and if it's not, it's not there. That's the way I decide.

WILDE: Then it's instinctive.

GREGORY: I key myself, my feelings, to their laugh machine. I've read a lot of stuff they would love coming from somebody else, but when I look at material, I have to look at it for me and bear my tone on the stage saying it. A lot of stuff I don't use. I throw away enough stuff from my writers to make ten million comedians in America because they are funny lines to begin with, but they're just not lines I can use.

WILDE: They don't fit you? They're not right for you?

GREGORY: Yeah.

WILDE: Is an education important for a comedian?

GREGORY: I would say it is. But there's so many outside elements involved in being a comedian.

WILDE: Like what?

GREGORY: Being aware of social problems and social conditions and of people. The more education you have, the better comic you'd be.

WILDE: Is a comedian born or made?

GREGORY: I think they are made. Of course, kids are naturally funny because they say things we adults would not say because of convention, society. My daughter was very hip as a little girl. Eight o'clock one morning I said to her, "Be quiet!"

"Well, Daddy, we gotta make a deal with you," she said. "If you're gonna go out and get drunk and come in with a headache and don't wanna hear no noise at eight o'clock in the morning, then you're gonna have to take us with you every night and get us drunk because it's normal for kids to get up at eight o'clock."

WILDE: Is there any luck in getting ahead, or do you have to make your own breaks?

GREGORY: There's luck in getting along in show business—just like any other business—but it's not luck to stay up on top. It's hard work . . . very hard work. Constant study. I read a great deal. But even more than that I have a research staff of twenty people set out to probe and get information.

WILDE: How important is a comedian's technique?

GREGORY: That's what makes him. This is the thing he could never sell. This is the thing that material can never do. You can take away the jokes, you cannot take away my technique. And if you do and you perfect it well enough, then you become a mimic.

WILDE: Is economic security an advantage to a comedian?

GREGORY: Yes, very much so. It allows him to chance material he knew was good but was worried about trying. When you go out on stage worrying about the laughs, or the audience laughing, then you get in trouble. They sense a certain insecurity. They are all there for the same thing . . . to have fun, and they gotta see that *fun* look. I don't like to use things that I know are safe. The challenge is to go out and use unsafe stuff.

WILDE: Doesn't that come when the comedian has achieved a degree of success and emotional security? Until then, he's still looking for the strong, powerful, big laughs.

GREGORY: When I walk out on stage, the audience is not a challenge to me. I don't go out there saying I'm going to make you laugh. I go out knowing they are going to laugh. Not as a threat but as a friend. It's like if I was at your house and asked you for a glass of water, I'd get it. It ain't a challenge. They know you're there. They came to see you. We're not against one another. . . . I'm not scheming against them, and this is the attitude I have.

WILDE: What advice would you give to a comedian just starting?

GREGORY: Go to the library and bookstores and get every book he can lay his hands on and read the jokes and learn as much about comedy as he can. The most important thing is not to be in a hurry. Doing comedy is like money in the bank. As long as you're good you never have to worry, as long as you are constantly growing while you're waiting for the break. Another thing is knowing people. Watch 'em. Look at 'em. Not just staring at them but figuring them out. There's no school to learn to be a comedian. It's trial and error. There's more facilities for a man to become president of the United States than to become a comedian. And we need good comedians just as much as we need good leaders.

MALCOLM

Malcolm X was tragically gunned down on February 21, 1965, during a speech at Manhattan's Audubon Ballroom. Gregory was deeply saddened but not the least bit surprised. The two spoke the night before Malcolm's assassination. They expressed great clarity that they were both being actively surveilled and both were government targets. Their friendship was initially delayed because Malcolm expressed doubts about Gregory's ability to balance his celebrity with the liberation of Black people. He felt Gregory's crossover celebrity status relegated him to the role of puppet or clown. However, upon meeting, they immediately became lifelong friends and allies.

Dick Gregory on Malcolm X:

—"The first time I met Malcolm, he was already with the Nation. At that time I was famous. I'm performing at a theater in New York. The phone rings. [Stern voice] 'Dick Gregory? This is Brother Malcolm. I want to know when you're coming to the mosque.' I said, 'Send a car. I'll come now. Get a photographer. I'll stand with you on the cover of [the Nation of Islam newspaper] *Muhammad Speaks*.' He calls me back a minute later. 'Brother Dick? Don't even think of coming here. You know you can't. Ninety-eight percent of your audience is white.' I said, 'I know. Malcolm, send the car.' He refused again. And that's where you see his playfulness, and his kindness."

They met at the mosque and posed for photographs.

—"Malcolm was John Wayne. Malcolm was all of my heroes. Malcolm came right out of every Hollywood movie. He looked them in the eye and said, 'This is the way we're going to deal with it.' And we loved him for that."

—"Malcolm was a sweet and bashful man, a kind man, and a good-humored man and someone who would be embarrassed if he could hear us talking about him in this way now."

Malcolm X on Dick Gregory, Audubon Ballroom (December 13, 1964):

—"Dick is one of the foremost freedom fighters in this country. I say that in all sincerity. Dick has been on the battlefront and has made great sacrifices by taking the stand that he has. I'm quite certain that it has alienated many of the people who weren't alienated from him before he began to take this stand. Whenever you see a person, a celebrity, who is as widely known and as skilled in his profession as Dick, and at the same time has access to almost unlimited bookings which provide unlimited income, and he will jeopardize all of that in order to jump into the frontlines of the battle, then you and I will have to stand behind him."

SPEECH AT VIETNAM DAY, UNIVERSITY OF CALIFORNIA, BERKELEY

(May 21–23, 1965)

Gregory publicly opposed the American war in Vietnam earlier than any other civil rights leader. After President Lyndon Johnson sent in the US Marines in March 1965, anti-war activists on university campuses began conducting "teach-in" protests of American escalation. One of the earliest and most important was at the University of California, Berkeley, in May 1965, where Gregory joined Dr. Benjamin Spock, Norman Mailer, and other prominent figures in questioning US foreign policy.

I called LBJ the other day to try to discuss the Vietnam crisis with him. Oh, I call him every now and then. It's very important to me because I'm going to be honest with you, I'm not about to fight them Chinese. When you stop and think China has something like 688 million folks—and I say *folks* because *people* might scare the hell out of you—and when you stop and think China got 688 million people, if them cats ever start singing, "We Shall Overcome," they gonna do it. You realize China got more census takers than we got people? Not only are there 688 million Chinese, but they're right down underneath us. And wouldn't it be wild if them cats very nonviolently decided to all get drunk at the same time and stomp their foot together? And what really knocked me out is when China blasted off their second nuclear blast and our State Department called it primitive. I called Dean Rusk that morning. I said, "Hey, baby!"

He said, "Greg, I guess I goofed again."

"You damn right you goofed, man. I wanna know how you gonna call China's nuclear blast primitive when you're scared of my switchblade!"

And then he informed me that it wasn't the nuclear blast that the State Department was referring to as being primitive. What he meant by that statement, he said, that through our intelligence—if that's what they want to call it—we have found that it would take China twenty to thirty years to develop the vehicle to deliver that bomb over here. That's what he told me. I said, "Man, do you realize with 688 million people, they can hand-carry that bomb over here?"

It's been said that we here know nothing about what's going on. Well, I'll tell you one thing, I don't know that much about what's going on, but I know last Sunday in Saigon the marines had a race riot. They did their best to keep it away from a lot of people, but it still made the papers. They watered it down a whole lot because when I first read the headline of the article and it said, "Marines Fighting in Saigon," I said, "Well they *been* fighting there. Hell, they must be trying to tell us something new." And I read it and it comes out they talking about a race riot. In Saigon. We had a race riot over there. And here's people saying this meeting's no good because we don't know what's going on. Huh? Well, I tell you what, if we don't know what's going on in Vietnam today, the government damn sure had enough time to tell us. And the only reason people from the State Department didn't show up here is because they know the only thing they would tell you, you weren't going to buy. . . .

There's a whole lot of people in the federal government that didn't like what's going on, but they have to put up with it because they haven't got crowds like you that's with them. And the larger these crowds get, the more people in the federal government gonna start screaming about all of these wrongs and these illnesses. Thank God for you.

Now, in closing, if you can be labeled communist, if the civil rights movement can be labeled communist, then they better go back and label Tom Paine as communist because all we're doing today is what Tom Paine said years ago in his "Wintertime Soldier": "If there be trouble, let it be in my time, that my children may have peace." No more, no less. Had your parents read Tom Paine thoroughly, we might not have to be here now. But they didn't. What you are doing here tonight, unborn kids around the world will be affected by it . . . if you don't stop! In our generation, we produced the mad man that created the nuclear bomb, or we produced the intelligence that created it, and the mad man got hold of it. And now he has contaminated the air with nuclear radiation, and you young, brilliant kids are gonna have to create a mind to vacuum-clean the air. And this is the best vacuum cleaner I've seen yet, what you're doing here.

As far as war, as far as the way that radical group will say, "Ah, they're just holding that meeting because they want to duck the draft." They'll always think of little petty things to say, but I tell you one thing, I'm not against armies as long as that's the army that's just gonna come in after the tornado and help clean up. I'm not against the army if it's the type of army that's gonna go around the world and distribute food to everyone. But I'd love to ask the boys in Washington, DC, how a Black can stand up and say he's nonviolent, and white America loves that, and is gonna send me over to kill somebody? No, nonviolence to me means not that I'm not supposed to hit an American white man. Nonviolence means to me that death might put me on its payroll, but I'll never put death on my payroll. So if America goes into a full-scale war, it's too late: nonviolence has captured me. But I tell you what, just so these little stupid groups wouldn't say Dick Gregory didn't go because he wanted to stay back here and make money, if I ever get drafted again, I'm going. But I'm gonna go and instead of the government making a deal with me, I'm gonna make a deal with the government. I'll go in your army, I'll sit through all your training under one guarantee: that when my basic training is over, you'll send me to the front line. And I don't want to take your gun with me this time. And if I can give my life on the front line for all of this wrong, I would much rather do that than kill a man, be I right or wrong.

Thank you so very much for being here tonight. God bless you. Hope to see you again real soon.

MARTIN

On April 4, 1968, Martin Luther King Jr. was shot and killed while standing on a balcony at the Lorraine Motel in Memphis, Tennessee.

I was in the State of California, campaigning for the presidency of the United States and lecturing at various colleges. Earlier in 1968, I had become a write-in candidate for the nation's highest office, with Mark Lane as my running mate. At a little after 4 p.m. that day [April 4], California time, I was driving with a friend to Hartnell College, where I was scheduled to deliver a lecture. Our conversation was interrupted by a radio bulletin. Martin Luther King had been shot in Memphis!

I began to remember Martin, clearly, vividly. I remembered his sweet innocence and his warm, gentle smile. I thought of the time when he and I had been riding on a plane and he expressed concern about my personal safety. "Now, Gregory," he said, "I want you to be careful. I'm just afraid they're gonna kill you."

I answered, "If they do, Doc, will you preach my funeral?"

He said, "I sure will."

We continued our drive to Hartnell College in silence. Numb and in disbelief. Finally, we arrived at the school. Standing up before an audience was the last thing I felt like doing that night. But, of course, I had to go out there and explain as best I could how I saw the situation. Many people were in the audience only because they wanted to know my thoughts and my opinions of the day's events. They knew Martin and I were friends and that I held him in great esteem.

At my lecture that night, I realized for the first time that America was in trouble with her young white kids. I was surprised to see the effect King had on them. They had grown up hearing about him, seeing him on television, and being influenced by his national presence. No matter what J. Edgar Hoover or their own mommas and daddies may have said about King, these young white kids knew he was not wrong and he was not bad. Martin was a living denial of all the racist myths perpetrated in the white community about Black folks. Martin didn't lie, he didn't cut, he didn't steal, and he wasn't on welfare. These young white kids learned some truths about Black folks from Martin Luther King, and he had a more profound impact on their minds and lives than anything they had heard around the family dinner table.

Martin Luther King had become a victim of violence while preaching nonviolence, and it raised a crucial question. When I heard the conclusive word of his death at my hotel that night, the question became even more compelling. Would the concept of non-violence, already under brutal attack by many Blacks and whites, die with King? Would Black awareness and Black progress be buried with him? Would the tremendous strides toward awakening the conscience of America to the plight of the poor and the oppressed be halted? Had Martin lived and died in vain? Was it possible that violence had conquered nonviolence?

For the first time since the news of King being shot, I smiled, a reflective smile, sad and bittersweet, and I recalled the words of

Gandhi: My creed for nonviolence is an extremely active force. It has no room for cowardice or even weakness. When a man is fully ready to die, he will not even desire to offer violence. History is replete with instances where, by dying with courage and compassion on their lips, men converted the hearts of their violent opponents. King had faced his attackers; he did not beg, or scream, or whimper.

Martin Luther King Jr. was laid to rest in the spirit which defined his days among us. It was a poor folks' funeral, as sad as it was beautiful. I knew then there would never be another Martin Luther King Jr. and, further, that there did not need to be. A little bit of Dr. King resided in the heart and soul of every American. He had awakened it and brought it out into the open. He did what he had been placed on Earth to do. There was no need for subsequent imitations of his life. America is a better place because Dr. King lived. History may prove him to have been his country's salvation.

Ironically, President Johnson was unable to attend Dr. King's funeral because he had to meet his generals and talk about Vietnam. Still, I imagine the president spoke from the heart when he said, "We are shocked and saddened by the brutal slaying tonight of Dr. Martin Luther King. I ask every citizen to reject the blind violence that has struck Dr. King, who lived by nonviolence."

I shall never forget the reaction of white America that night. The looks of horror, disbelief, embarrassment, and guilt. The haunting question was written on every face: "How will Black folks react?" I saw it on California governor Ronald Reagan's face on television. Black folks in California saw it too, and I really believe his tearful expression of personal shock and horror was largely responsible for keeping things cool in Watts.

The account of the assassination printed in the *New York Times* was typical of the press response throughout the country: The thirty-nine-year-old Black leader's death was reported shortly after the shooting by Frank Holloman, director of the Memphis police and fire departments after Dr. King had been taken to St. Joseph Hospital. "I and all the citizens of Memphis," Holloman said, "regret the murder of Dr. King, and all resources at our and the state's command will be used to apprehend the person or persons responsible." The police broadcast an alarm for "a young white male," well dressed, who was reported to have been seen running after the shooting. Policemen poured into the area around the Lorraine Motel on Mulberry Street where Dr. King was shot. They carried shotguns and rifles and sealed off the entire block, refusing entry to newsmen and others.

Dr. King had been in his second-floor room throughout the day until just about 6:00 p.m. central standard time (7 p.m. New York time). Then he emerged in a silkish-looking black suit and white shirt. He paused, leaned over the green iron railing, and started chatting with an associate, Jesse Jackson, who was standing just below him in a parking lot. Mr. Jackson introduced Dr. King to Ben Branch, a musician who was to play at a rally Dr. King was to address two hours later.

As Mr. Jackson and Mr. Branch told of Dr. King's last moments later, the aide asked Dr. King: "Do you know Ben?"

"Yes, that's my man!" Dr. King glowed. They said Dr. King then asked if Mr. Branch would play a spiritual, "Precious Lord, Take My Hand," at the meeting that night. "I really want you to play that tonight," Dr. King said.

The Rev. Ralph Abernathy, perhaps Dr. King's closest friend, was just about to come out of the room. A loud noise burst out. Dr. King toppled to the concrete passageway floor, and blood began gushing from a wound. Someone rushed up with a towel to stem the flow of blood. Rev. Samuel Kyles of Memphis placed a spread over the fallen head of the Southern Christian Leadership Conference. [Kyles was to have hosted a dinner for King and his associates that night before the rally.] Mr. Abernathy hurried up with a larger towel.

And then the aides waited while policemen rushed up within minutes. In what seemed to be ten or fifteen minutes, an ambulance arrived. "He had just bent over," Mr. Jackson went on bitterly, "I saw police coming from everywhere. They said, 'Where did it come from?' and I said, 'Behind you.' The police were coming from where the shot came."

Mr. Branch, who is from Chicago, said the shot had come from "the hill on the other side of the street." He added: "When I looked up, the police and the sheriff's deputies were running all around. The bullet exploded in his face."

"We didn't need to call the police," Mr. Jackson declared. "They were here all over the place."

COINTELPRO

COINTELPRO was a covert counterintelligence program conducted by the FBI from 1956 to 1971 to discredit and neutralize organizations considered subversive to US political stability. It often used extralegal means to criminalize various forms of political struggle and to derail several social movements, including those for civil rights.

May 15, 1968

A confidential memorandum from FBI Director J. Edgar Hoover directed to the Chicago FBI office said, "Gregory has traveled all over the country preaching black nationalist extremism, hatred, and violence. . . . Chicago should review Gregory's file and his current activities to develop counterintelligence designed to neutralize him. This should not be in the nature of an exposé, since he already gets far too much publicity. Instead, sophisticated, completely untraceable means of neutralizing Gregory should be developed."

July 2, 1968

The special agent in Chicago wrote Hoover in response, saying, "The Chicago office has organized a counterintelligence 'team,' made up of SAs [special agents] experienced in RM [racial matters] and SM-C [security matters-Communist] Investigations, including

SAs with lengthy prior counterintelligence experience. This group, together with the RM supervisor and the SA responsible for the coordination of this program, have devoted considerable effort to methods of inhibiting the effectiveness and credibility of Gregory. His file has been thoroughly and exhaustively reviewed to this end. Chicago is continuing to give the matter of discrediting Gregory top priority, and bureau authority will be promptly requested ... in the event a specific counterintelligence device is formulated."

March 10, 1978

A decade later, Dick Gregory responded: "Do you realize what you have here? This piece of paper [the Hoover memo] has the director of the most powerful police agency in the history of this planet proposing to contact the Mafia so 'they could work together.' Look, if the FBI was going to contact La Cosa Nostra and if the FBI knew who they were, why weren't they arrested? . . . What I was saying was that one day we were going to find out that one of the most dangerous men in this country was J. Edgar Hoover, and we would probably find out that Lyndon B. Johnson was one of the worst tyrants. . . .

"I've been knowing the FBI has been following me and tapping my phones for some time now. In fact, whenever I wanted to get a message to Hoover, I just put it on my phone."

WRITE ME IN

Recognizing that the focus of the movement was shifting from the open, legal segregation in the South to the systemic racism and inequality in power structures around the rest of the country, Dick Gregory joined demonstrations addressing issues ranging from open housing and better schools in northern cities to the long-standing inequality imposed on Native Americans. He decided a more directly political effort was necessary in his adopted hometown of Chicago, so in 1967 he ran against Richard Daley, the nation's most powerful mayor. He won less than two percent of the vote, but the experience proved a useful lesson in the value of a protest candidacy.

The money from speaking engagements provided for my growing family, while I worked my way back into the political arena. This time I was going to run for president of the United States.

I would run again as a write-in candidate, but this time I would be smarter: we'd take our own pencils. *Write Me In* became the title of a book I wrote during my campaign that explained my reasons for wanting to be president of the United States. I received a $100,000 advance that I used to finance my campaign, which was very costly. The first thing I vowed to do if elected was paint the White House black.

There are only two things needed to qualify to run for president: you must be at least thirty-five years of age, and you must have been born in the United States. I met both qualifications, so the race for the highest office in the land was on. But my next move almost landed me in jail. I produced a photocopy of a $1 bill with my face on it instead of George Washington's. My running mate Mark Lane's name was also on these bills. Mark is a longtime friend, a respected attorney, and a former member of the New York Legislature. He authored *The Rush to Judgment* about the Kennedy assassination, a book that totally destroyed the conclusions of the Warren Report. Before the book was published, the FBI mounted a smear campaign against him. Because of J. Edgar Hoover's interference, Mark's book was initially refused by all the major publishers in the United States. His book was published in England, and it became the number one bestselling book worldwide. I was proud to have him as my running mate and to place his name on the dollar bill.

I had gotten the idea one day when Lil and I were delivering food to some people in need in Mississippi. Another couple had driven down from Illinois to meet us to help with the food drive. A brick had been thrown through their window because, like all Illinois drivers, their license plates read "Land of Lincoln." But they couldn't get rid of the $5 bill that has his name and face on it. That's when I realized the power of money.

I thought my photocopy dollar bills were a great publicity idea, but the US Treasury Department didn't agree. It made the news. And not just any news, mind you—there it was, big as day, on the *CBS Evening News*. Walter Cronkite held up one of my bills with a blown-up image of the dollar bill behind him. The Secret Service confiscated my campaign literature under direct orders from the Treasury Department. They claimed the bills were working in change machines all over the country, and they were. But Cronkite said on the air that the money was tested at the CBS news station in the snack-room canteen and it did not work. Now if Cronkite said it, then "that's the way it is."

Eventually, the Feds had to return our money because we found out there was a federal law that said any photocopy of American money was a violation of the law. Well, our answer to that was, until you put a Black person's face on American money, nothing that has my picture on it is a copy of American money. So they gave us the money back, and we continued our campaign.

My bid for the presidency came to an abrupt halt at 6 p.m. on April 4, 1968, when Martin Luther King Jr. leaned over a balcony at the Lorraine Motel in Memphis, Tennessee. He was talking to some of his supporters below when the assassin pulled the trigger and gunned him down.

A little more than a month after Dr. King was assassinated, Bobby Kennedy was assassinated on June 6, 1968. I did not go to Bobby Kennedy's funeral; I went to jail instead. I was at home in Chicago listening to the radio when I heard that I had lost my appeal and had been sentenced to ninety days for a 1966 arrest for illegal fishing (for Indian fishing rights) in Washington State.

When I was released from the Thurston County Jail, I went back home for a few days before I got back on the college circuit and the campaign trail. The candidates for president in 1968 were Richard Nixon, Hubert Humphrey, George Wallace, and me. The press was as clever then as they are now, and that worked to my advantage. The media was calling me daily asking for interviews. They really did not want to hear about my desire to paint the White House black, let alone any of the more serious issues on my platform. It was all about equal time regulations. They knew that George Wallace and other candidates would demand equal time if I were to appear on their shows.

I lost the war, but I won the battle. My campaign had given me the opportunity and forum to discuss issues that affected Black and oppressed people, and that was more important to me than winning. After the election of Richard Nixon, I declared myself "president in exile," and we planned two inaugural balls in Washington, DC. One ball was held at the Hilton, and the second at American University. Several weeks before the ball, George Wilkins, president of American University, abruptly canceled our ball because he said there was insufficient parking available. God stepped in and so did the faculty and staff at American University. The American Association of University Professors and the Organization of Afro American Students openly supported me. The chairman of the student group wrote, "In specific terms, the question is Gregory, but generally it is whether students will be trusted with themselves. This university is racist. We feel that Gregory is important to the nation. We're talking about the hunger right here in Washington. What if the people were to eat up everything in sight? What if they became human locusts? This time they might come up past Connecticut Avenue."

The articles written about the American University cancellation had the same effect on my visibility as the interviews had on my campaign. We finally received permission to have the ball. And what a ball we had! My vice president in exile, Mark Lane, wasn't able to attend because he was in New Orleans working with District Attorney Jim Garrison on the Clay Shaw case. Shaw had been charged with conspiracy in the assassination of President Kennedy. Mark couldn't leave New Orleans, so attorney Jean Williams swore in Lane via telephone. I was sworn in by attorney Ruby Burrows at the ball. We thought about calling Billy Graham, but it was Reverend Jim McGraw who opened our ball with a prayer. After the swearing in ceremony, we went over to the Hilton, where the second ball was in full swing.

The crowd at the Hilton cheered as their president in exile took the stage. Lil and I danced all night, shuttling back and forth between the two balls. The evening was so perfect I almost forgot that it wasn't real. I wondered what Mama was thinking as she watched the ball from heaven. She now knew that Richard and Dick were the same person, her son. The next morning, when I looked in the newspaper, there we were—Lil and I—on the fourth page of the afternoon paper.

IMAGINE: BED-IN FOR PEACE, MONTREAL

(June 1, 1969)

Rock stars John Lennon and Yoko Ono conducted a weeklong anti–Vietnam War protest in a Montreal hotel room in the summer of 1969. International media took in the scene as invited guests discussed the peace movement and helped record the song "Give Peace a Chance." It was here that Dick Gregory shared a nondenominational prayer book with Lennon that helped inspire the song "Imagine." Gregory's conversation with the couple was captured in the film Bed Peace.

We have to do the one thing that the unions did to bust the establishment—that was organize. Charge your dues and say, "As a member, I will not represent you [the union]. We will represent poor folks." And then the system crumbles. The system falls. It doesn't fall at the tone of a gun, or at the tone of violence, but at the tone of [people] being lifted up. The bad part is when the system falls, usually you've got to rebuild. This way we rebuild it as it's falling because this whole system, as we know, has to go. We put emphasis on property rights instead of human rights, and the day that we get a movement across the world going that human rights is the number one thing we are concerned about, then you get a different bag. It's like in America, we tell American kids how beautiful democracy is, but you've got to ask yourself the question, "If democracy is so damn good, why do we have to go all over the world trying to ram it down people's throat with a gun?" The day we make our democracy work right for the first time, that's the day we'll put the guns down, because anything good you don't have to force on people. They'll steal it.

I was always hung up with my church that told me I couldn't kill a man that broke into my house and raped my wife and daughter. But the state could kill them, and the church never told the state not to. So I felt they were picking on me. When you look at the scene in America, when you get the electric chair, the last person you see is the priest or the minister. You could wipe out capital punishment in the morning if you took this film crew here and went up to a man who was getting the electric chair, and said, "If you would let us film this all the way through, we could guarantee your death would wipe out capital punishment in America." You go in and you film him, then you tell everybody that the Beatles are going to do a special, Christmas Eve, and tell everybody in America, "Don't eat. Plan your meal around the special." Then the special comes on at 1 and when they show that cat gettin' it, nobody will want to eat. The whole country will be outraged because the last thing we get to see in America is the minister. That's our symbol of capital punishment.

This is where people will say, "You're doing it for publicity!" Morally dedicated entertainers have to do things for publicity, as long as it is morally pure. In America we've used publicity so badly. . . .

John Lennon, 1980

"Dick Gregory gave Yoko and me a little kind of prayer book. It is in the Christian idiom, but you can apply it anywhere. It is the concept of positive prayer. If you want to get a car, get the car keys. Get it? 'Imagine' is saying that. If you can imagine a world of peace, with no denominations of religion—not without religion but without this 'My god is bigger than your god' thing—then it can be true."

PART III

THE SPIRIT

(1971–2017)

Dick Gregory's meteoric rise to fame and fortune was intentionally cut short. Funds were diverted and priorities reassessed. The civil rights movement had awakened his spirit. Metamorphic change abounded: the athlete-turned-entertainer became an activist, health guru, and social critic. The wind at his back, Gregory was a sole practitioner now. Gone were all of the lettered organizations that once aligned with and prioritized his agenda; he was on his own. He left the nightclub circuit for the clean air and sober audiences of collegiate lecture halls.

Red carpets gave way to grassy yards and gymnasium floors. This was where he was destined to be. Lil and their ten children were safe and thriving on an organic farm, light years away from North Taylor and all that it represented. His comedic timing remained razor-sharp. His weapon now was his ability to make you laugh and strategically drop a truth bomb to rattle your beliefs. The self-described agitator was ripping and running, shaking up and agitating the world, adding the Vietnam War, nuclear power, and South Africa's apartheid government to his list of causes.

Carrot juice replaced whiskey, and vegetables replaced meat. He was a shadow of his former self—a shadow that was far from done. After all, he was certain that the star the mystic woman saw on his head was not the star of show business but the sign of a lifelong activist teaching people how to live and let live.

—CHRISTIAN GREGORY

MY ANSWER TO GENOCIDE

(October 1971)

Dick Gregory had never been afraid to ruffle feathers and counter conventional thinking. This 1971 Ebony editorial challenged new concerns about global overpopulation and addressed long-standing fears of birth control being imposed on Black Americans as a form of genocide. Two months after publication, the magazine's editors noted that "letters from readers continue to flood Ebony's offices about the article." Two years later, a historian of the topic called it "probably the best-known single article on the subject of birth control and Blacks."

My answer to genocide, quite simply, is ten Black kids. Now I know that statement is going to upset a whole lot of white folks, and even some Black folks. More and more white folks these days who are interested in ecology and overpopulation ask me why I have such a large family. Hell, I had six kids before white folks started getting concerned about ecology. Now Planned Parenthood groups are saying that a couple should have a maximum of 2½ children. I'm still trying to figure out that half a kid. I know my American history well enough to know what "three-fifths" of a man is, but half a kid?

I guess I never will understand white folks. Now they're trying to tell us how many babies we should have. But I'm one Black cat who's going to have all the kids he wants. White folks can have their birth control. Personally, I've never trusted anything white folks tried to give us with the word "control" in it. Anything good with the word "control" in it, white folks don't want us to have. As soon as we started talking about community control, white folks went crazy.

I guess it is just that "slave master" complex white folks have. For years they told us where to sit, where to eat, and where to live. Now they want to dictate our bedroom habits. First, the white man tells me to sit in the back of the bus. Now it looks like he wants me to sleep under the bed. Back in the days of slavery, Black folks couldn't grow kids fast enough for white folks to harvest. Now that we've got a little taste of power, white folks want us to call a moratorium on having babies.

Lillian Gregory, December 1, 1971

"I, myself, am from a large family. There were fourteen children, and I remember growing up in Willard, Ohio, as a very happy time. There were seven boys and seven girls, so of course there was a lot of work, but there was also lots of fun. And we were poor. With our family today, it's just great, and we don't have to worry about where our next meal or money for the kids' schooling is coming from."

Michele (1959), Lynne (1961), Richard Jr. (1963 d.), Pamela Inte [Satori] (1964), Paula Gration (1964), Stephanie [Zenobia] (1965), Gregory (1967), Miss (1968), Christian (1970), Ayanna (1971), Yohance (1973)

On March 18, 1964, one year and three days after Richard Jr. was born, Lil gave birth to Paula and Pamela. We gave them the middle names of Inte and Gration so they would always remember their mother's suffering when she was jailed during pregnancy while fighting for civil rights. My oldest son, Gregory, has just one name. His birth certificate does not read "Gregory Gregory," but rather simply "Gregory." In the American system, whose computers, bureaucracy, and institutional requirements demand two names to function, my son Gregory is a symbol of independence of the built-in entanglements which predetermine the destiny of the "two-namers" in a controlled society. At the time of my seventh child's birth, racial hang-ups in the United States made it difficult for some white folks to call a Black woman "Miss" and a Black man "Mister." So to be on the safe side, my wife and I named our daughter Miss. All her life, anyone who calls her by her proper name will have to say, "Miss Gregory."

THE CIRCUIT: UCLA SPEECH

(January 27, 1972)

From 1968 on, Dick Gregory's preferred audiences were college students, and by the 1970s, lectures on campuses across the country were his primary source of income. This 1972 talk at UCLA is a good example of the way Gregory used his trademark wit and social commentary to challenge and inspire young people to improve their troubled society and care for their own well-being.

Student Host: Good afternoon. Sorry, we're a little late, but we had a little difficulty: the plane came in late. As chairman of the Associated Student Speakers program, I'd like to welcome you to our third program of the winter quarter. We have with us Mr. Dick Gregory, who as of today is in his twelfth month of fasting. He's eaten nothing, he only drinks, and it's pretty hard to do. He's just come out with a new book, and we'll skip the rest of the introduction since we're a little bit late. It gives me great pleasure to introduce a warm human being and a great man, Mr. Dick Gregory.

I would like to say thank you very much. Can you people back in the cheap seats hear okay?

Twelve months ago, I vowed I wouldn't eat any more solid food until the war was over in Vietnam. The reason I mention that to you now is because in case the war should end today, in the middle of my speech, I have a clause in my contract that says all I have to say is "bye, y'all." Let me briefly discuss fasting with you. The hardest thing about a long fast is the dumb, stupid questions the eaters keep asking. Like after going ten months without eating any solid food: "How do you feel?" And when you tell them "hungry," they really act surprised!

I guess one of the big hang-ups with me on fasts is the people that are close to you. Whenever you go on a long fast, they really think you're going to die, but naturally, they won't say anything to you about it. They just start acting kind of strange. Like, you can't borrow money from them anymore. . . .

Let me clear up one thing. There's a lot of people that believe the number one thing that preoccupies all men's minds is sex. Well, I say to you, if you believe sex is the number one thing that preoccupies your mind, you try giving up eating. Your old, rotten, scrawny, beat-up half a turnip lying in a garbage can right now would make a fool out of a whole trainload of women to me.

I changed planes in Chicago this morning and flying in, I'm sitting next to one of them eaters. I'm sitting next to one of these cats that like leaps into his food, right? He's sitting there eating and reading the *Playboy* magazine. So when he gets to the center page, he nudges me: "Anytime you see something like this, what does this make you want to do?"

I said, "As hungry as I am, it makes me want to put an apron on her and send her out to get me something to eat!"

Whenever you go on a long fast, it's always good to kind of psych yourself out ahead of time, kind of program yourself. Like say,

"Now I'm going to lose some weight." My top weight at one time was like 288 pounds. I'm down now to about ninety-eight. And you just keep getting your clothes taken in. I've had these pants taken in so many times, the left pocket's on the right side. It really gets embarrassing when you go to buy underwear. I mean, I don't mind shopping in the children's department, but the diaper section does kind of get to you, you know.

Now something that really just kind of gets to me—as many times I've been on a fast, I always fail to realize that anytime you go on a long fast, you automatically quit going to the toilet. And that's a right I'm just not ready to give up. I mean, I get some of my best thinking done in the toilet. So I still go. I had a fifty-five-minute layover in Chicago changing planes this morning, so I went to the toilet. One of them weird cats followed me in, and goes like this, "I thought you wasn't eating!"

And I said, "I'm not!"

He said, "Well, what are you doing in the toilet?"

I said, "I'm rehearsing!"

Something that really kind of bugs me is pay toilets. Don't that kind of get to you? I mean, it's got to be the mark of a sick system that's going to charge you to . . . You ladies have pay toilets? I wonder if they're like how in the men's room we have all pay toilets and one free one. Is yours the same way? And the way they bill that free one, you wouldn't *dare* go in there!

I don't know, I guess the whole world's gone crazy.

I guess I can truthfully say I spend about 98 percent of my time today on college campuses for a reason. The simple reason is you young folks in America today are probably the most honest, ethical, dedicated, committed group of young people that's ever lived in the history of this country, bar none. And I just hope you youngsters don't have to continue to read all them right-wing, cracker-controlled newspapers to find out who you are or what you all about.

You see, the average established newspaper in America today is not even morally sound enough to discuss you young kids. They call you hippie, yippie, irresponsible, bearded, smelly kids—whatever that means. My reaction: because you have a beard, why does that mean you have to stink? They didn't say anything about Abraham Lincoln. He didn't only have a beard; he was ugly too! I guess what I'm really trying to say is, I hope you youngsters in America today understand who you are and what you're all about.

You know, one of the sad tragedies of America is the newspapers. In a free democratic society, it is very important that the press informs the masses and that way your society can stay free and democratic for a long time.

The sad tragedy in America is the press doesn't inform anymore. They are so busy selling ads; they haven't got any space left to tell you what's going down. What I'm trying to say is when you live in a society where the press is supposed to inform but does not, it's very important that you young folks devise means of informing yourself. Because if you don't, you're going to end up in a lot of trouble.

It's a shame that a Ralph Nader, on his own, a private citizen, got to tell me that the automobile industry ain't making nothing but deathtraps when it's really the United States government's job of protecting me against them slimy, degenerate freaks that manufacture automobiles. And I just cannot believe that no newspaper in America was hip to what was going on until Nader exposed it.

If the newspapers were really pulling your coat to the grocery stores and the chain stores in this country, 98 percent of everything they sell in the supermarket you'd know is unfit for human consumption. But how can they pull your coat to the foods that you eat, when they're running full-page ads from Kroger and A&P? Newspapers should have informed you a long time ago that 98 percent of all the chickens on the market are cancer infected. Not because they're born that way; it's the new process they use for getting them to the market by injecting the hormones into them, which knocks six weeks off the growth time.

What I'm trying to say is you better devise means of informing yourself. That's very important. When you go to the store to buy something, just read the label. And if there are any words you don't know what they mean, don't eat it. Pick up a product in the grocery store that says "color added." That's one step short of saying paint. Pick up a jar that says "strawberry jam," then right under that it says "imitation." Now you know the word *imitation* wipes out the word *strawberry*, so that means you're not eating strawberries at all.

Yeah, the press has really turned its back on informing folks. If the press had informed the average American of the fact that the CIA is probably one of the most vicious, degenerate, insane organizations that's ever been put together in the history of man, most Americans would be hip to the CIA. Instead, today they're so dumb they think the CIA is something good. But we'll find out when they overthrow this country, and have no doubt about it, at the rate they're going, they're going to overthrow it.

You've got a big job. And you haven't got much time.

It's very important that you youngsters spend a little time and study how Hitler came to power. I don't mean what he did after he got in power, most folks know that, but understand how he came to power. It was a whole lot of terror acts committed in Germany and blamed on other folks and using the fear of the masses. You've got to check out some of these newspaper articles you've been reading lately. You might find out we're on the same parallel.

You young people in America need to find a means of informing yourself. Please understand who you are and what you are all about. Don't depend on the establishment to decide and determine you and your efforts, because they'll blow it every time.

They proved that last year at the May Day demonstration. Most of these freaks didn't understand. Probably one of the grandest days in the history of America was the opening day of the May Day demonstration. Seven thousand folks went to jail—never before in the history of America had that many people been arrested in one day. What did they go to jail for? Snatching pocketbooks? No. Selling dope? No. Seven thousand folks went to jail because they dared come to Washington, DC, and sit down in front of a bridge to try to create a situation to force Nixon and the rest of them slimy, degenerate freaks in the Pentagon to end that vicious, insane war in Southeast Asia.

Oh, I wish I was young enough to get drafted. I wouldn't go to Canada. I wouldn't go to jail. As soon as I got my induction notice, I'd hurry up to the Pentagon and say, "Send me to the front line immediately . . . on one condition. You have to send me to the front line with some rich folks." That's right. I ain't going nowhere with no poor folks. No, I've been around poor folks all my life. I know how poor folks act when they get scared and think they're gonna die. They go, "Oh, Lord!" Little rich white kid gets scared and thinks he's gonna die, he says, "Mother!"

In four days of demonstrations in Washington, DC, they arrested 13,800. For the benefit of those Americans that didn't understand what happened, maybe they should check out the arrest slips. They'll find out that 99.9 percent of those 13,800 were draft age. It shouldn't be too hard for them to understand what happened: a group of young people came to Washington, DC, and sat down in front of a bridge to try to create a situation so they wouldn't have to sit down in front of a bullet. To be honest with you, if we raised the draft age in America today to seventy-five years old, there'd be a lot of freaks sitting in front of bridges in the morning.

I told my wife, "You realize Washington, DC, Police Department has got to be the most brilliant police department that's ever existed in the history of man?"

She said, "Why?"

I said, "Do you realize how brilliant you got to be to arrest seven thousand people in one day, and don't get one criminal?" I mean, you got to be trained to do that. How do you arrest seven thousand people in one day and don't arrest one pimp?

I tell you why. Because all at once in America today, we have decided we know what the criminal looks like. Long hair, beard, sideburns, mustache, T-shirt, sandals. That's him, get him! You know, Christ would fairly well be in trouble if he ever decided to come back to America today.

Every major metropolitan police department is doing something wrong. The syndicate hoodlums—everybody knows who they are—but they can't go to jail. How do you think dope pushers and prostitutes can work right out on a street corner without the help of the police? I got off the plane today at about 11:30 and I arrived here at 12:15. I could leave you right now, and within fifteen minutes' time, go out and find me some heroin, some reefers. Do you believe that? Now ask yourself the question, how can I come in here from Chicago, haven't been here fifteen minutes, go out and find the heroin man, the reefer man, but the Los Angeles Police Department who lives here, works here, was born here (some of them), they can't find the same man? There's something wrong.

Black folks aren't telling you something we read in no book, something we saw on television. We're talking about something we've lived. That ghetto is a heck of a trip. We hip to the police structure. At five years old in St. Louis, I knew what the whore looked like. I knew what a pimp looked like. Five years old. I knew what a hustler looked like. I knew what a bookie looked like. I knew what a dope pusher looked like. At five years old, I couldn't believe I was that much smarter than your police. Six years old, I see the cops standing on the corner patting the whore on the rump. Six years old, I see the cops standing on the corner laughing and telling jokes with the pimp. Six years old, I see the cop stick his head through the car window where the dope pusher's sitting.

Well, I'm not six years old anymore. I'm thirty-nine years old, and I keep hearing white folks in America saying, "Have respect for the local police." And we say to you, "You got to be sick, insane, and out of your mind." If my own mother's behavior pattern was the same as your police structure, I wouldn't have no respect for Mom. Every sick, slimy, degenerate in the Black community that serves as a detriment to Black folks, that white racist police structure lets him function unmolested by the arms of the law. But when my beautiful Black leaders come into the ghetto—I'm talking about my Stokely Carmichaels and my Rap Browns and my Angela Davis and my Martin Luther Kings and my Malcolm X and my SNCCs and my COREs and my NAACPs and my Black Panthers. I know a lot of white folks hate to hear those terms, but we wonder why those pimps and whores and dope pushers don't upset you the way my beautiful leaders do. The same white racist police structure seems to wipe out my beautiful leaders one by one by one by one.

We're sick and tired of it, and we're going to deal with it too.

I say to you youngsters that every major problem confronting

America today was created by man. Which means these problems can be solved overnight if you young folks decide to solve these problems with honest, ethical statesmanship, and not this sick, tired, degenerate political muscle. Stinking, slimy, degenerate forces are now telling us they can solve the problems. You're darn right—they created problems. The Democrat and Republican Parties are unfit to govern this country anymore.

You youngsters have got your new right to vote. You better get hip to it. You eighteen, nineteen, and twenty-year-olds, you better realize one thing. If I give you the right to elect, but don't give you the right to select, I still got you working out of a trick bag.

You youngsters mess around, you'll end up making the same mistake we Americans have made the last one hundred years. Every time we go to the polls, we end up voting for the lesser of two evils. Try that for one hundred years. One day you end up with the evil of the evils.

You young people got to form independent political action, so for the first time in the history of America, statesmen can enter the political arena instead of politicians. In times of crisis, statesmen flex their minds, while politicians flex their muscles.

You got a big job.

You got to make these so-called educational institutions for the first time live up to their name. You've got to make these so-called educational institutions educate you instead of indoctrinating you. There's a difference, you know, but anytime you live in a country that puts property rights ahead of human rights, it's only normal. They teach you how to make a living instead of teaching you how to live. Anytime you live in a country that's motto is "Let the buyer beware" instead of "Let the seller be honest," that country ain't long to be in existence. Anytime you tell a three-year-old kid going into a confectionery to buy some jellybeans that he better beware because the seller don't have to be honest, y'all in trouble.

If your grade schools and high schools and colleges and universities were teaching you how to live, about your body, nobody would have to tell you about alcohol and narcotics. I beg you don't forget about that body. Learn how to take care of it. If you can't learn it in these institutions, you better go to a health food store and get them books on raw food and vegetarianism. Get your thing together, 'cause until you clean out your body, you'll never get your mind together. And once you get your mind together, you can deal with all your problems. As long as you eat all that garbage that keeps your body fouled up, and your mind fouled up, you're so busy dealing with those six basic fears—fear of poverty, fear of getting old, fear of getting sick, fear of death, fear of losing your love, fear of criticism—that you can't deal with nothing else. I beg you youngsters, learn about that body. Get into raw food and vegetarianism, and just try it for six months or three months and see how good you feel. As you purify that, you purify this country.

You got a big job.

You got to deal with jail reform. You got to deal with the police powers. You've got to understand that the number one and number two most important people in any free democratic society are the fireman and the cop. We don't pay them nothing and tell them their job's so important they can't even strike. You give a man an important job and treat him like a dog, he'll bark for you one day; treat him like a pig, he'll oink on you one day.

You youngsters got to deal with the old folks in this country. You've got to understand that anytime the reward in any society of getting old is a lonely old folks' home, that nation has gone mad and maybe beyond the point of no return.

You youngsters got a big job.

What Black folks are talking about today in America, so few people understand what we're saying. You know, what really baffles Black folks in America today is white folks' reaction to us: "What's wrong with them? Niggers done gone crazy!" You know, to be honest with you, niggers got more sense today than we have had in the history of America. And when niggers was basically crazy, that's when most white folks thought we had good sense, running around, goosing my rump, and rubbing my head for luck.

When niggers were really crazy, white folks understood us. Niggers running around pressing their hair to make it look like white folks' hair; you thought we had good sense. Now, niggers just let their hair grow out natural, the way nature meant for it; all at once we're militant now. As long as we were looking like you, running around the street, chocolate-covered white folks, you thought niggers was good. That's when we were crazy. A Black woman running down the street with a blonde wig on, that doesn't scare you at all. That should scare you to death!

As long as niggers walk around looking funny and acting strange, you dig that. When we reach back to the normal flow of nature, everybody gets uptight. You really messed up niggers' minds; now we are trying to get it together. That's why we're talking about Black studies, talking about Black awareness. Yeah, we're trying to get our thing back together.

If Black folks were acting the way we're reacting in this country today for no reason at all, we would truly be crazy. But Black folks are reacting the way we are today simply because America is the number one most racist, oppressive system on the face of this Earth. That's what we're reacting to. A lot of white folks in America fail to realize one thing: that the same universal intelligence bank that put white folks' heads together also put Black folks' heads together, and it's my universal intelligence that's making me react to these insults.

We're tired of these insults, and all we're doing is dealing with them—no more, no less.

I beg you youngsters to understand how strong you are and understand something else. Nixon should never get on television and tell you when he's going to end the war. You're strong enough to get on television and tell him when he better end it! If you use your strength, you can end that war in any given thirty days.

That's what my fast is all about. You don't fast to change the hearts of tyrants. You don't fast to make bad people good people. You fast to organize all the ethical forces together. When that power comes together, the bad forces got to move over. The bad forces have controlled this country for four hundred years, and for the first time, we've got enough good force to get together and say, "Move over chump, we're coming through!"

You youngsters, understand your power now. Nothing affects this country more than when you clamp down on the Jolly Green Jesus. You tried everything else, and it didn't work. You tried burning American flags. These freaks will manufacture more American flags in one hour than you can burn in ten years. You tried carrying the Viet Cong flag. They'll manufacture more Viet Cong flags than you can carry. That didn't end it. Jump on this dollar, try that.

You organize and call for a nationwide boycott of General Motors products in this country until the war is over in Vietnam. What do you think would happen? The chairman of the board of General Motors does not have to go to Washington, DC, and sit in front of a bridge to get Dick Nixon's attention. The chairman of the board will get on his private jet in the middle of the night, fly to

Washington, DC, get there at 4:30 in the morning, run all the way down to the White House, kick the gate open, stomp them two Secret Service agents out of the way, run across the White House lawn, jump through Nixon's bedroom window, run up to Nixon's bed, kick Pat out the bed, reach down and grab Dick Nixon in his pajama shirt collar, and snatch him out of the bed and say, "Boy, you let that war in Vietnam affect the stock of General Motors, and we will run you out of the world!" You personally make a commitment that you will not buy another General Motors product until the war is over, and write your friends.

You youngsters got a big job. The fate and destiny of this country depends on you. You young white kids in America, let me briefly thank you for changing our civil rights movement into a human rights movement. Because of you, for the first time today, we talk about our Chicano brother. We talk about our Puerto Rican brother. We talk about our Indian brother. For the first time, we're talking about women's rights in America. There's a lot of people who think the women's liberation movement is a jive game. A lot of folks thought the civil rights movement was a jive game, woke up one day and found out we were real. You're going to wake up one day and find out the women's liberation movement is real.

As I leave you, I say to you youngsters, you got a big job and not much time. I know it's going to upset a lot of you, but I beg you to understand that violence is not the answer. If violence was the answer to solving problems, as violent as America is, we could solve all the problems on the face of this Earth in two days. America wants you to be violent. It programs you to be violent. If it can get you simple enough to end up with a shotgun, and she's standing with a missile . . .

That's what the cowboy movies are all about. Why do you think a seven-year-old child can go to any movie in America and see a cowboy shoot 'em up, kill 'em up, but he can't go see a love story where there's no killing and murder? Why do you think the number one television show in this land for fifteen years has been Matt Dillon [*Gunsmoke*]? Once a week that sick, perverted pimp rides through your living room. Shacking up with Kitty. Fifteen years that chump ain't changed outfits. He wears the same thing, and you don't care because he kills good.

We program little kids. You don't believe that? Any of y'all ever look at those cartoons on Saturday morning? Those of you that haven't, I beg you to get up Saturday morning and look at those cartoons on television. Bugs Bunny, man, you see more dynamite being used in a Bugs Bunny cartoon than you'll see on all the war films coming back from Vietnam for the next three months. Sounds funny to you, but it ain't funny to them kids. That's a plant there. You plant it, it'll grow, and you got to reap it one day.

Violence is not the answer. For every gun you can come up with, America's got a tank. For every stick of dynamite you got, she's got a missile. The one thing you young kids have that America can't deal with, the one force you have that she can't match, that's your moral force. And I beg you youngsters in America today to rally behind morality. Rally behind that moral force. Understand that when you muster an army together that's willing to die for what is right, you will frighten the death out of an army that's willing to kill for what is wrong. You got a big job. You don't have much time.

FROM STAND-UP COMIC
TO LIE-DOWN MARTYR

(August 15, 1972)

By the early 1970s, Dick Gregory was increasingly difficult to catego-rize as a public figure. While he continued to perform as a comedian and join civil rights and anti-war demonstrations at a moment's no-tice, he also embraced new causes and new forms of protest. In this 1972 World magazine interview, he explores the connections between his seemingly disparate roles after more than a decade on the public stage.

GREGORY: Just about all the positive names I'm called in the press, I would answer to. I'm a comedian, an activist; I work in civil rights; I'm a father, an author, and a lecturer.

INTERVIEWER: What do you consider yourself to be primarily?

GREGORY: A statesman, I guess, if I had to sum it up. A statesman is a person who would, in dealing with the masses and the groups, make the right decision because it's the honest, ethical decision and not a political decision.

INTERVIEWER: Have you ever wanted to be anything but a comedian and an activist?

GREGORY: I grew into these things. You come up in a racist system, and the oppressed take on the characteristics of the oppressor. So I wanted to be everything the white folks wanted to be. I wanted to be Buck Jones, the cowboy, the Lone Ranger. I wanted to be all of the things that represented manhood in a sick society. It just so happened I hit it big in show business around the time the civil rights movement spilled out into the streets. I was a celebrity, and they were looking for celebrities to raise money at benefits and what have you. I'm just tickled to death that I was born at the time I was because very few times in the history of man do the powerless attack the powerful.

INTERVIEWER: Did you ever want to be wealthy? Was that one of your ambitions?

GREGORY: When I was a kid, yes. You see, I was on relief for twenty years. What wealthy was to me is not what wealthy is to most people. Wealthy to me was picking up a paycheck every week. And when I got into show business, at the Playboy Club, and they told me they were going to pay me $250 a week, I thought that was all the money in the world. And when I went up to $5,000 a week, I didn't believe it. I still don't believe it. Once I got interested in comedy, I fought to work. I was working three days a week for three years, and just the fact, man, of being able to work five, six days a week was all I wanted. People said, "You can make $50 a night."

"Wow, six nights a week, that's $300." I couldn't conceive of there being much more money in the world than that.

INTERVIEWER: Did you also have trouble when you were making it, managing your money? Did you fall into what might be called the Joe Louis syndrome, with money running through your fingers?

GREGORY: A lot of people think something happened to Joe Louis. I think it was groovy. I think to be born Black or poor white in America, you owe yourself $200,000 worth of treats just to un-mess up your mind. It cost me a whole lot of money just to get my-self mentally to where I could deal with the world. In a white racist system, man, it works. I had to go all the way around the world be-fore I found out things. I had to go to Africa to find out that Black was beautiful, to see the way Africans walk, the respect they have for one another—all these things that the Tarzan movies taught me were negatives. There are a lot of Black people in America that made money and kept money and have not done anything for the cause of humanity. I think Joe Louis has done a lot for humanity, mainly because he was able to use the money to fulfill things in his head that this country just doesn't fulfill for poor Black folks.

INTERVIEWER: You have cut heavily into your show business ca-reer to pursue civil rights and peace activities. Do you have an esti-mate of how much money you voluntarily gave up in this pursuit?

GREGORY: One guy really documented it by taking an adding ma-chine and figuring up the dates I lost compared to the ones I had, and he came up with well over $1 million.

INTERVIEWER: If that's accurate, do you have any regrets about it?

GREGORY: None whatsoever. What I got in my head—the mon-ey's bad now anyway. You know, Rolls Royce stock went down to 3 cents a share in one day. But what I got in my head, man, can never be devaluated.

INTERVIEWER: In the last few years, you've practically given up nightclubs in favor of the college lecture circuit. What were your ideas in going on the circuit, and what did you hope to accomplish?

GREGORY: I realized about five years ago that the power of this country was there in the form of ethics and integrity and honesty and just raw statesmanship looking for direction. So I went to the college campus, and when I got there, I realized that's where I want to stay for now. Thanks to the young white kids of America, the civil rights movement was changed into a human rights movement, and now for the first time we're talking about the Indian and the Black and the Chicano. We're talking about poor white folks in Appalachia and about the Asian American. That's where we are now, and I would say it is directly an outgrowth of what happened on the college campuses.

INTERVIEWER: It has been said that you and Ralph Nader and Julian Bond are the speakers most in demand on the college campuses and probably, on a year-in, year-out basis, the most highly paid as well.

GREGORY: I do about three hundred lectures every ten months, whereas Julian Bond has got to be in the legislature and Ralph Nader has so much time he has to spend with his groups. I probably should be well paid if I wanted to. I could go for $3,000 to $5,000 per lecture. I wouldn't work as many schools because if you go for $5,000, you can make $10,000 in two engagements. Whereas my minimum is $1,000; my maximum is $1,250 to $1,500, depending on how far the distance is. I deliberately keep my price down so I can get to small schools.

INTERVIEWER: Do you see a common link between you and Nader and Bond that makes all of you attractive at this particular time on the college campus?

GREGORY: Honesty, integrity, and the ability of young kids to appreciate this. They want to hear the truth, and they want to be involved with things that they feel are good. There are no scandals on us.

INTERVIEWER: Isn't it also at least partly the fact that all three of you attack the establishment in one way or another and are, under certain definitions of the word, radical? Do you think that has anything to do with the attraction?

GREGORY: No, because the Rennie Davises and all those cats that attack it stronger than we do are less sought after than we are, so if that was the attraction, there'd be a whole lot of people like them still on the college campus. I'm not knocking them. I'm saying that you have to have more than that to be a repeat on the college campus.

INTERVIEWER: Julian Bond says that in his travels around the colleges he finds essentially no difference between students at Harvard and at a junior college and that the questions he gets in one place are at the same level of intelligence as another.

GREGORY: Yes, it's like I'm standing in one room and all the kids are coming to me. It's hard to know whether I'm at the University of Alabama or UCLA. Like five years ago, when I went to the University of Montana—that's Missoula, Montana, man—and they knew everything that was going on in the world. The social thing runs just as strong in Missoula, Montana, as it runs in Chicago or in Greenwich Village, New York.

INTERVIEWER: On white southern campuses, have you had any difficulty in recent years? Or is it the same there now as any place?

GREGORY: No difficulty there whatsoever. There's a good law now that the educational system has that if any speaker is denied the right to speak on a college campus, that college can lose its accreditation. So maybe a lot of people would react, but they don't because of that.

INTERVIEWER: What are you telling the nightclub audiences, which are mostly not of the college-age group?

GREGORY: At the nightclub, I'm there to entertain; at the college campus, I'm there to inform. But I'm like a doctor. I wouldn't sit around and talk about how to cure cancer to people who are drinking alcohol. It's the same thing with the social problem. I'll march if necessary; I'll go to jail if necessary, but I don't come to nightclubs to make a point or to put a message across. I happen to be a social satirist, and I stay as close to what happened in the newspapers from a social point of view as I can. But that's all.

INTERVIEWER: Do you have a vision of America as you would like to see it?

GREGORY: I'd like to see us in America love America a little bit less and respect the United States Constitution a little bit more. Because I see the same thing happening in America that I see happening in many love affairs: one party cheats on the other, and eventually the marriage can't hold up. We cheated on America far too long, and the marriage can't hold up.

INTERVIEWER: What type of national leaders would you like to see in this country?

GREGORY: Roy Wilkins of the NAACP; Ralph Abernathy, SCLC; Ralph Nader; Murray Kempton. I'd like to see Fannie Lou Hamer in the presidential campaign. I'd like to see Janet McCloud—a really humane person I met on an Indian reservation—Dr. Spock, Jane Fonda. There's a tremendous amount of people who have gone out of their way to be their brother's keeper. They'd do it if they were in a position of leadership, so that twenty-four hours a day they could dedicate their energy in the government to solving the problems of mankind.

INTERVIEWER: Mr. Gregory, I'd like to talk to you more about Black politics. Can you place yourself in the Black political spectrum somewhere between, let's say, the Panthers on one hand and the Urban League or the NAACP on the other?

GREGORY: The system tries to put people in bags, and it's very difficult to put somebody in a bag when all of them are talking about the same thing. The Black Panthers, the Urban League, the NAACP, Malcolm X, Martin Luther King have been talking about putting somebody in office who is going to see to it that the Black folks are relieved of the racist conditions that affect their jobs, their schooling. If you go fishing with a net, and I go with a hook, the important thing is that we're fishing. The unique thing about the Black movement is that all of them are talking about liberation. It is just a difference in tone, and you're always going to get this. You get one guy much older, and he might be much wiser. You get another guy who's young; he might be hipper. The riots never ceased until the Panthers came on the scene because what most Americans failed to realize is that there were a whole lot of young dudes out there who had just got out of the army or just got out of jail, and there was no group they could join. There were a whole lot of people who didn't believe that the church was the answer. There were lots of people who looked around and wanted to be a part of the movement, but they had criminal records; they were on drugs. The Black Panthers came around and said, "My brother, you on drugs, man. My brother, you ain't got no job, come on over here."

The whole thing started changing. The energy that was used to relieve frustration by throwing bricks and firebombs was now being used to relieve frustration by feeding my brother, by going in and saying, "We've got to set up the type of mechanism that will get some urine tests to find out how many of them young Black kids in the Black community got lead poisoning." Ironic as it seems, the government takes programs that the NAACP develops—they don't say that they took it from there—and they also take programs that the Black Panthers have developed; for instance, a hot food program for people other than kids in school. But what about my baby, man? You're going to check the urine of a kid in the fifth grade, but what about the kid before he comes to school, man? That's when the big wipeout happens.

So the Black Panthers were on the scene. If you called the Black Panther headquarters and said, "Brother, it's cold here and my kids don't have coats," the Black Panthers would be on the scene with the coat. So I guess the NAACP could do without the Black Panthers and the Black Panthers could do without the NAACP, but the masses can't do without either one of them.

INTERVIEWER: Two of the touchstones in discussing the Black movement used to be whether a person or a group would sanction the use of violence and would be willing to work within the system. How do you feel about that?

GREGORY: If I go in the army and learn how to be a pilot and drop bombs on people, that's working within the system. If I decide to be a policeman and carry a gun and kill somebody that's robbing a place, that's violence working within the system. A cowboy movie, man, is working within a system. So are all of the violent books we put out; nursery rhymes that tell me Jack and Jill went up the hill, but before the nursery rhyme is over, both of them are going to fall down. Humpty Dumpty can't sit on a wall without falling off. Little Miss Muffet can't sit on a tuffet without a spider scaring her away. You look at the basic principles of the American way of life. It's violent. And nonviolence, to me, goes far beyond the United States Constitution. Nonviolence gets into the universal order.

The United States Constitution tells me I got a right to have a gun in my house and blow your brains out if you enter. Now I don't believe that I have a right to kill you under any circumstances. I'm also a vegetarian. I would never knock a steak off your plate. Don't want you putting no pork chops on mine. In a violent nation, I think it is normal for people to be reacting violently.

As a kid, I used to point my finger like nothing—"Bang, bang." I used to sit in my window, man, and draw a bead on people on the street like I had a rifle and go, "Bang, bang." I learned that in the movies, man; there are no guns in my house. You know that in this country, I am permitted at seven years old to go see a cowboy shoot-'em-up, kill-'em-up movie by myself, but they won't let me in to see *Love Story* with no killing and no murder, and so I would say America is a violent country. I hate to see violence, but I understand it.

INTERVIEWER: Is your type of comedy important to the political movements in which you are active?

GREGORY: I wouldn't say so at all. You know we didn't laugh Hitler out of existence. And there will be a cure found for cancer, only it won't be good humor. I think humor gives the individual who's oppressed the strength to carry on, but that doesn't come from comedians. That comes from me and you in the coal mine together—laughing, man, about all of this stuff in our lungs. This is what the songs came out of—the coal-mining songs, the Irish songs, the slave tunes. This is what helps me make another day, man. It's the humor that you and I can sit down and talk about as entertainers. Now entertaining helps relieve certain pressures off your mind, so for a few minutes, the elements of the universe can react to you the way they were supposed to react to you. That's why people feel good when they leave a good show. That's why they feel good when they leave a good play. Entertainment relaxes them enough that they forget about the rent; they forget about the deadline for a split few minutes. This is all I see myself doing as an entertainer. But when I go and give lectures at colleges and universities, I'm not playing games.

INTERVIEWER: Aside from being an entertainer, do you consider yourself a Black leader, and if not, do you think you could become one if you wanted to?

GREGORY: I guess I would have to be considered a Black leader, maybe, because I've been involved with the movement and maybe because I've out-survived so many of the other folks you know. The Rap Browns and the Stokely Carmichaels are gone. But I look at myself as a person that has graduated from the civil rights movement to the human rights movement. A social critic, I think that's where I fall mostly. I get more press about the things I say about the social order; I make my living saying things about it. If something happened that affected society and I didn't come in on it, a lot of people would be disappointed.

INTERVIEWER: You also do a lot more than simply comment, though. You've probably, as Martin Luther King used to say, made your witness in more places than any other person in the United States.

GREGORY: Well, the historian will be able to sit down one day and assess my role much better than I can. All I'm saying is that as long as I've been in the civil rights movement, I've never created a negative. And there are a lot of people who are not in the movement who just stand on the side and criticize, and that's very bad. As an American citizen, I chose to get involved. None of my involvement has ever been a violation of the United States Constitution. For me to get involved didn't take a great act of manhood. There are a whole lot of people demonstrating around the world that don't have a constitution to guarantee them that right. I'm doing it within the law and sometimes you go to jail, but I don't know if I would have been strong enough to do it if the Constitution hadn't said I had a right to do it.

INTERVIEWER: From time to time you have sounded ambivalent on the basic question of white people. I've heard you be quite harsh about whites—not only about individuals, but also the group—but on other occasions I've heard you praise whites of goodwill, commend one white leader or another.

GREGORY: I've always been harsh on the white racist system. If all the white folks left in the morning and no one was here but Black folks and we ran the country the same way white folks are running it, I'd be critical of that. This is my hang-up, you see: the system, the institutionalized racism that exists. I can understand George Wallace. The system made him. He didn't come down from outer space. He's a homegrown American boy. And I'm just sorry that he didn't come on the scene earlier because I'm glad that all those bitter white folk have something to rally behind other than my head. I know the more George Wallace talks and the more the white racists seem to freak out on what he is saying, the more they leave me alone, man. You know, we haven't had a Black cat lynched that we know of in years, so maybe the problem was that we didn't have the George Wallaces on the scene.

Now in talking about a white racist system, we often don't use the finesse we should use to describe the hurt. That's the beauty in a little kid: a doctor can give you a long, drawn-out thing about what is wrong with the kid, and the kid says, "Dad, I just got a sore toe." He locates what's bothering him, and he points to it in his own innocent way. That's beautiful, and I think it is what the minorities are now doing the world over.

INTERVIEWER: How do you feel about Richard Nixon?

GREGORY: Well, I tell audiences that when Nixon decided to mine Haiphong and made everyone think it was going to be World War III in the morning, then for the first time it dawned on me that I'd vote for George Wallace because I'd just as soon have a bigot in the White House as a fool. I could find it much easier readjusting to slavery than picking cotton in a radioactive field. White folks forget quickly. The same man who is telling them that he's the law-and-order man is the same man that stood in front of the schoolhouse to block law and order. That's why the Black folks say, "We're not interested in law and order; we're interested in justice." Once we get justice and once this country is about justice, it'll be a whole other ball game.

INTERVIEWER: Let's talk about you as a humorist. Do you agree with one writer who said, "Being outrageous is Gregory's style? Being funny is his craft and, of course, his business"?

GREGORY: I think that's probably true, but I don't go up to be outrageous; I go up to be funny. Some of the things I say are outrageous because we live in an outrageous time.

INTERVIEWER: Do you consider your stock-in-trade will be jokes about what might be called the Black condition?

GREGORY: Whatever happens to be current in the newspaper is what I talk about on stage. When I hit big in 1960, the Black problem dominated. Nobody knew what a Chicano was; nobody was interested in Puerto Rican problems or what the women's liberation movement was talking about. When the Congo situation broke out, every day for eighteen months there was a picture of a Black man on the front page of all the American newspapers. We moved into an era when Black men had to be reckoned with, an era when Black was coming into white folks' homes. These conditions were being exposed to the masses for the first time, so you could make a satirical situation out of them.

INTERVIEWER: Do you think this was a greater factor in the change in "Black comedy" than the onset of the civil rights movement?

GREGORY: It was all part of the picture, but the change started way back in '59 with the Congolese situation. Communications were very important too: the civil rights movement was brought right into your home. You're sitting down trying to eat dinner, man, and look across a bridge and see a lot of kids being tear-gassed. It became an everyday thing. Dr. Martin Luther King came on the scene, and whether you liked him or not, he had to be reckoned with because he was there.

INTERVIEWER: In both the comedy routines and the college lectures, I take it you've broadened your material a good deal. Do you now consciously include "Black material"?

GREGORY: Definitely. I go out of my way to work it in. That is still the number one pressure point in this country. If the Indians started marching in the morning and controlled the airways and the press, then the biggest bulk of my stuff would be about the Indians.

INTERVIEWER: Your fasting seems to fascinate everybody who hears you. Why do you think fasting is a particularly appropriate means of expression for you, and how effective do you think it is in changing conditions?

GREGORY: It's effective to me because I'm dedicated to nonviolence. I would rather be killed by a man than kill that man myself. I believe that anytime you muster an army together that's willing to die for what's right, you frighten the death out of armies that are willing to kill for what's wrong. The number one most mighty weapon in the nonviolent arsenal is fasting. You don't fast to change the hearts and minds of tyrants. You don't fast to make bad people good people. You fast to create a rallying point where all the honest, ethical forces can gather.

I had a priest call me today. I don't have time to meet with anybody, but I've got to meet with him because he's talking about a group of people in the church who are ready to start fasting until the war is over, even if it means dying. I had a friend of mine just come back from Hanoi, where he interviewed American prisoners, and the first question a pilot that's been confined for five years asked is, "How's the health of Dick Gregory?" This is the power of fasting. Gandhi is a fascinating example. I'm sure the British would much rather have dealt with him had he mustered an army because at that time the British army had the greatest army, the greatest navy existing, and he couldn't have won. I'm sure the British thought he was going to starve to death, and many of them wouldn't have cared. But it gave the Indians such a powerful force, such a rallying point, that the British had to get out of their country after 150 years of occupying it. That's the power of fasting.

INTERVIEWER: What are the roots of your commitment to this type of activity? Was it Martin Luther King, or does it go back beyond that?

GREGORY: It grew from Martin Luther King. When I joined the nonviolent movement, I wasn't nonviolent. I was scared. If Martin Luther King said, "Come down to Mississippi and march," I assumed that I had a better chance of not being killed than if Malcolm X said, "Come down with your gun." I wanted to go with a gun. At the time I thought that everybody down there needed to be wiped out. And going then appealed to my cowardice. But when I became truly nonviolent, I realized that you have to be a coward to want to kill somebody or hurt somebody because violence is a tremendous form of sickness. I'm just tickled to death that the movement afforded me the opportunity to be exposed to a way of life that's honest, that's ethical, and that's worth dying for. Before I was exposed to a way of life that was dishonest, that was unethical, and that was worth killing for.

INTERVIEWER: Fasting and nonviolence have deep roots in Eastern cultures, and I notice that in your nightclub performances you refer to numerology; that's in part Oriental, and it's also occult. Is there any particular fascination in the Oriental and the occult for you?

GREGORY: No, my fascination goes to the universal order. There are nine planets in the universe, and we have nine holes in our bodies, so I believe we are all small replicas of the universe. One is the sun, so if you're born on the first of June then your soul number is one and you're affected by the sun. I've been able to take numbers and figure out my destiny. I can look at a person, put his hands a certain way, hold his head a certain way, and I know what numbers he has in his birth chart.

I've been able to use it mostly as a safety valve because I got the CIA and the FBI and all those freaks running around under the false pretense that I'm a threat to America's security. So they use that false pretense to know every move I'm going to make. But the CIA and the FBI and these other clandestine organizations that run around watching me and other people who are for right in this country— they are the ones who are a threat to us. We're not a threat to America whatsoever. And so I can use this; I can get on a plane and I know what a man looks like who's got a three in his number. I know what a man looks like who's got a gun on him because he holds his head a certain way. I know how cold steel works with certain numbers—the balance number—because you're dealing with chemistry now. That's why the English people are so hip. They don't let the cops carry guns because they know once you put a gun next to you, you're going to get lead poisoning. Your body is a living, breathing organ, and anything close to it is breathed in.

And so there are tremendous ways of being able to tell, especially when you fast, because you purify your body, and your body tunes in. How does a dog know when you and your partner are walking down the street as kids and the dog is a block away and you say, "When we get down here, let's kick the dog," and the dog moves. He didn't hear you. He's tuned in to the universal force. If your body is in order, you can tune in to any message that's negative to you. This is what cleaning your body out is all about.

INTERVIEWER: You mean you literally use numerology as a sort of counterintelligence weapon?

GREGORY: Sure, and fasting too. It's totally impossible for any of these freaks to kill me now. It's a simple law of nature; the stronger the man, the closer the assassin. And the cat that's out to kill has got to get so close to me I can deal with him. Look at General de Gaulle. You know how many times they shot at General de Gaulle and couldn't kill him? They were too far away. That's true of knives, any kind of weapon. So all you've got to do is be in tune and watch your back.

INTERVIEWER: How does that work in the case of a man like Martin Luther King? He was certainly strong, but he got shot from a distance.

GREGORY: You've got to understand that Martin Luther King was hit by the government. Was he shot from that distance they say he was shot from? There's one school that says in order for him to have been shot from there, somebody would have had to come and move a tree that was in the direct path of the bullet.

INTERVIEWER: What is the exact nature of your diet? I've read that you do eat some raw vegetables and fruit.

GREGORY: No, I'm a fruitarian. Haven't eaten vegetables in two years. For the last fourteen months, I've been taking fruit juices and water. Nothing solid to eat at all.

INTERVIEWER: So you don't have anything to chew on at all. Do you miss the chewing part, the oral satisfaction as it is sometimes called?

GREGORY: Yeah, I miss that, but you don't miss anything as much as you miss the taste. That's what we're hooked on. Not on food—on taste.

INTERVIEWER: It seems as though the combination of long-distance running and fasting would be devastating to your body. What does the doctor say about that?

GREGORY: I don't check with doctors. When I go out and run ten, twenty miles every day, I'm the doctor. When something's wrong, I find it out quickly. It would be wrong if all I took was water. But there's tremendous nutrients in juice, as long as it hasn't been cooked. I travel with a juicing machine, and 98 percent of the juice I take is fresh juice. This is what is called live food, and you get all the nutrient value you want out of it.

INTERVIEWER: In your years in the civil rights and peace movements, what is the most dangerous situation you've ever been in, and what is the most dramatic or moving situation?

GREGORY: Probably the most dangerous situation was in Watts when I saw the police coming around the corner. Somebody was shooting outside a housing project, and there were kids playing and I put my back between the cops and the kids so they wouldn't shoot. I did get hit in the leg, but it was from the inside, from whoever was shooting at the police. But I'm at the level now where nothing scares me.

I think the most dramatic one was when we carried twenty thousand turkeys down to Mississippi for Christmas back in the mid-sixties. To look at the people's faces, to hear the woman say, "I'll be thinking 'bout you when I fry this," because she never had turkey before. It was beautiful.

INTERVIEWER: If you had to sum up what the movement has achieved in all the years you've been in it, would you say you're satisfied with the achievement?

GREGORY: Definitely. I'd say that where we are today, the civil rights movement has turned into a human rights movement. For the first time, we're talking about everybody's problem.

CAUGHT IN THE ACT:
FINAL NIGHTCLUB PERFORMANCE

(August 5, 1973)

EMCEE: As many of you no doubt know, this is a very special and historic night in the history of show business and in the almost legendary life of Dick Gregory: his final nightclub performance. Dick Gregory, a decade and a half ago, opened the nightclub doors for so many of his fellow comedians. And now tonight, after this performance, he closes that door behind himself. And I think that a telegram from another close friend, Steve Jaffe, says it very well: "No man has given more, asked less, or been more needed. A decade and a half of wit, insight, knowledge, and entertainment was your gift to us. As you go on to other service, we thank you, and dedicate ourselves to returning your gifts in kind to your chosen beneficiary, mankind." And so tonight, August fifth, at 12:11, here at Paul's Mall, United Artists proudly presents the one and only Dick Gregory.

In fifteen years, I've made millions of dollars, went all over the world, financed all my schemes, been further one way, thanks to nightclubs, than most folks will ever go round trip. . . . Why am I giving it up? Well, I'll tell you why. I will be forty-one years old this coming October. And thanks to the civil rights movement, thanks to the peace movement, and all of the beautiful people I was able to meet because of my involvement on a worldwide level, at forty-one years old (to be), I know now that there is a universal force that controls the whole thing. You can call it anything you want to call it. But one day, it is going to balance out all of our ledgers, and it's going to be a simple question. Not how much money did you make, were you funny, did they like you, were you a celebrity, who was your mother, who was your father, where did you live, what school did you go to, where did you send your kids to school. . . . It's gonna ask one simple question. And all of us are gonna have to deal with it. How much service did you give to your fellow human beings? Just that simple, and just that sweet. No more, and no less. And that's really weird, because we won't be able to say, "Well, you know them racists, man, wouldn't let me get no education." No, man, how much service did you give to your brothers and sisters? How much service did you give to your wife and your family? How much service did you give?

Nightclubs keep me up until three or four in the morning, and it cuts down on the amount of service that I'm able to give the next day. That's the main reason I'm leaving. I have a conflict going on college campuses, and I do about three hundred lectures every year, saying that drugs and alcohol are bad for you. 'Cause it really wipes me out, the mentality of Americans, to put down reefers but never down alcohol. And, I mean, I can't understand. . . . Do anything you want to do, but don't—because a few powerful white folks in New York City said alcohol is legal and didn't say reefers was legal—put one down and praise the other. Because we're gonna get into a lot of trouble in this country. I find a personal conflict in saying to them young kids, "Reefers and alcohol is bad," and then say, "Hey, come on down to the nightclub and catch my act, and have a drink." So that's a personal thing with me. It's not the main reason, it's the minor reason.

And so, let me say tonight as I leave you: thanks everybody, and to United Artists, who's putting this on tape so I'll always have it.

In closing, America is caught up in Watergate. A lot of people are upset, don't know which way this country is going. There's a couple of positive things that came out of Watergate. When 200 million people in this country thought that we weren't going to get to the bottom of Watergate, one man, by the name of Judge Sirica, said, "It ain't going this way." One man. That happened to be appointed by Eisenhower, so he didn't have any party hassles. And now we're getting to the bottom of Watergate. One man. And we've heard this, down through the years, that one person with courage is the majority. Martin Luther King Jr. proved it. Malcolm X proved it. Medgar Evers proved it. And all the people that got involved in the civil rights movement proved it. And there's another good thing that came out of Watergate. A lesson we should have learned a long time ago. I guess they will always remember it in Europe, but anytime you get people that's in control of a nation, any nation, that talk about law and order and never talk about justice, there is a Watergate somewhere close by.

So, as I leave you, I say to you and to America—with Watergate breaking around us, all of the foul, degenerate things we're finding out this country is involved in—there's a new age coming. Yep. There's an age coming that's not too far away. This age is going to be beautiful. This age is going to be where honesty and ethics and integrity will be the cornerstone of this nation. And I say to the Indians, and the Chicanos, and the Puerto Ricans,

Asian Americans, to the women, and to Black folks, the poor white folks, there's gonna be a new age in this country. An age where justice and liberty and freedom for all is going to be praised one day the same way we praise wealth in this country today. And I say to you there's a new age. An age where nature is going to control this country. And so, as I leave you, I say to you, may peace and understanding be with you now and forevermore. May peace be with you, my friends. Thank you.

THE JFK ASSASSINATION:
GOOD NIGHT AMERICA

(March 6, 1975)

Dick Gregory became a vocal advocate for a more thorough investigation of the assassinations of John F. Kennedy and Martin Luther King Jr., particularly as troubling covert actions on the part of the FBI and the CIA were uncovered in the 1970s. Gregory helped increase the pressure for a deeper exploration of Kennedy's death with a 1975 television appearance on Geraldo Rivera's Good Night America, *during which the Zapruder film of the assassination was broadcast for the first time.*

RIVERA: How did you get involved in this and in the circumstances concerning and surrounding the death of President Kennedy?

GREGORY: I've been involved with it since the first day accidentally. I was at home when the news came over the wire that President Kennedy had been shot. I thought that had we had radio and the communications systems when Abraham Lincoln was shot, how valuable would tapes be, in 1963, of Lincoln's assassination? So I put on all my radios, all my televisions, and started taping. About four hours into taping, I started hearing the same people being interviewed again, and what they said the first time had changed. The only common denominator was that they had talked to the Secret Service. From that point on, I was a little suspicious of what was happening.

I started listening to the theory that Lee Harvey Oswald was the lone assailant, and then things started coming out that we didn't know before. That the parade route had been changed, and that Lee Harvey Oswald—the day that President Kennedy made the announcement he was going to Dallas—got a job at the book depository. If the parade route wasn't going that way, then he had set himself up in the wrong location. Or he knew something. Now if Lee Harvey Oswald did not have the ability, and the power, and the rank and position to change the parade route, then who did? From that point, I started really looking into it. I met a very brilliant gentleman in London at the time named Ralph Schoenman, who had also been looking into it. I started meeting various people that were looking for something else. I found out that there was a whole . . . like occult out here that didn't believe it, but we just kept looking and kept waiting for the press. Then when they said they would have the Warren Commission, this stopped everything because we knew that these loose ends would be tied up, and they never were.

RIVERA: Aren't you frightened sometimes that someone's going to try and hurt you?

GREGORY: No, I tell you, I have a wife and ten kids, and if something happened to all of us, America is bigger than we are. And if the assassination of President Kennedy is reopened, and the truth is found out, my family and myself are very insignificant. What scares me the most is the amount of decent American people who have called me, who have sent me letters, who meet me in airports and say, "Wow, I heard about what you're into. They are going to kill you!" The fact that we live in a free democratic society, and in our subconscious we admit that there is an organization that will kill you . . . I would say that I'm outraged—not at the CIA, not at the murderers. I'm outraged over the fact that the American press should be doing what we are doing today.

There are thousands of researchers that have as much, if not more, than what you heard us say. We were just fortunate enough to wiggle it through and slip it to the American people. I would like to see the American press, even the press that says everything we have is not true, come out and do the research and let the American people know: Was it a trick? Was it a conspiracy? Let's open up the Warren Report. Let's talk about a new investigation for the two hundredth anniversary of America. If we don't, I think this country's going to be in a lot of trouble.

A WINNING FORMULA

At the peak of his comedic career, Gregory's lifestyle of smoking, drinking, and eating the wrong foods resulted in ulcers and headaches, and at 288 pounds he was grossly overweight. Determined to achieve optimal health, Gregory turned to veganism and devised a nutritional plan that included a supplement he created called the 4X Formula. In 1976, he ran fifty miles a day for seventy-one days—seven million steps—from Los Angeles to New York, sustained only by his 4X Formula and juice. The formula evolved into Dick Gregory's Slim-Safe Bahamian Diet, with sales exceeding $113 million in just two years. In 1989, he purchased a beachfront hotel in Florida to use as a health, nutrition, and weight-loss center. The Bahamian Diet was the longest-running product for General Nutrition Center in the 1980s. Thousands of multilevel distributors were employed by Dick Gregory Health Enterprises Inc. His ultimate goals were to teach health and financial independence.

My diet had been completely meat-free for nearly two years. I would love to say that in those two years I had become the picture of health, but that would be the furthest thing from the truth. There are many ways to abuse your body outside of eating meat, such as smoking, drinking, and eating junk food. I employed each and every one of them.

One day a buddy of mine said, "Hey, I've got someone I want you to meet." Since I was planning to run for mayor of Chicago against Richard J. Daley, I assumed he meant someone politically connected who could help my campaign.

We pulled up to a little health food store on the South Side, where we were greeted by the shop's owner, a lovely lady in her late fifties. Her hair was tied up in a scarf, African-style. Her smile lit up the room. "This is Dr. Alvenia Fulton," my friend announced, "the world's foremost nutritionist and natural healer." See, I told you poor nutrition shows. It must have shown up on me to the point that my friend took it upon himself to bring me to this health food store.

She invited us in and immediately began doing what she loved most—sharing her vast knowledge about food and nutrition. I listened, but I wasn't buying any of it. No milk? Anyone with an ounce of sense knew that milk made strong bones. No white bread? Come on, lady, I thought to myself. Everybody and their mama knows that Wonder Bread builds strong bodies eight ways. For everything she said, I had an answer. I was always told that vitamins make you fat, and here this lady was telling me to take vitamins when I knew I needed to lose some pounds. I really knew she had it backward when she started talking about fasting. Go without food for more than a couple of hours?

"Did Mayor Daley tell you to suggest I starve myself?" I asked. The quizzical look on her face said she had no idea of what I was talking about. The bottom line is I was a very misguided, misinformed individual. Thankfully, Dr. Fulton didn't give up on me, and eventually her wisdom and guidance helped change my mind and my life.

When I began to protest the Vietnam War, I wanted to do something very dramatic to bring my activism to the world's attention. By that time I had visited Dr. Fulton's store a couple of times, and some of her wisdom was beginning to sink in. She told me about the beautiful aspects of fasting, and how it had brought her to another level, spiritually and mentally as well as physically. "How about a fast?" I told myself. "Are you nuts?" Self said back. Well, maybe.

The next day I stopped by Dr. Fulton's and told her about the fast I was about to undertake. "I'll be drinking nothing but distilled water," I said, half expecting her to say that would be too drastic of a move for my first time fasting. Instead, she said, "If you're really serious about this fast, I'll go on it with you." And she did. I don't think I would have made it through that first fast without her guidance and counsel.

First, she told me to prepare myself by cleaning my body out with enemas and then drinking only freshly juiced fruit juices for seven days prior to starting the fast.

The media played my fast up as a "hunger strike." Ultimately it was more of a "healing strike." Although I fasted for forty-one days and lost nearly 190 pounds, and I sometimes felt like I was going to die, my body was probably in better shape than it had been in twenty-five years. Dr. Fulton became my best friend, my adviser, my mentor, my guide, my nutritionist, and my motivator. Whenever I felt down or hungry or like I was going to die, I called Dr. Fulton, and she reassured me. She even told me everything that was going to happen, day by day, on the fast. She told me that in the third week of my fast, I'd get an amazing "second wind." That's exactly what happened. I had more energy than I had when I started. That's because by the third week of fasting the body begins to consume itself, and it gets all of the stored-up poisons and waste that have been occupying your body for years out of your system.

Dr. Fulton also cautioned me not to break the fast by starting to eat everything at once. She told me that after a long fast, a person must drink nothing but one eight-ounce glass of fruit juice for every five days of the fast. Since I fasted forty days, I had to have eight days of juice before I could start eating normally.

Dr. Fulton had made me a believer. Years later, she and I collaborated on a book, *Vegetarianism: Fact or Myth*. I was also an occasional guest on her radio program, *The Joy of Living*.

I began fasting as an instrument of protest, and although fasting has its benefits, long periods of fasting can ultimately harm the body by robbing it of the essential nutrients needed to thrive. When I speak of long periods of fasting, I'm not talking about going from breakfast until lunch without eating, or skipping lunch and waiting until dinner.

If you do decide to fast, make sure you're doing so under the supervision of a qualified health practitioner. Fasting under Dr. Fulton's supervision improved my health and gave me a new lease on life. I had stopped drinking and smoking. I felt good enough to start running again. Running is something I have always enjoyed, so I really didn't need a reason to jump back into it. However, I got some good reasons to run, whether I was looking for them or not.

The more I learned about healthy eating, the better I felt. The better I felt, the more I hungered for more knowledge about this wonderful gift mankind possesses called "nutrition." I now understood the philosophy behind eating to live as opposed to living to eat. I absorbed every bit of health information like a sponge. I couldn't get enough. Name a city and I could tell you where the health food stores are located. I visited them all and always headed straight for the book rack. I literally have hundreds of thousands of health and nutrition books in my library, and I have read every one. However, my quest for knowledge took me far beyond just reading books. I began to attend classes, workshops, and seminars. Of course, my greatest teacher was Dr. Alvenia Fulton, and I absorbed every morsel of her precious wisdom. I also learned a great deal from Dr. Roland J. Sydney, a world-renowned naprapath who became our family physician. Like Dr. Fulton, he was passionate about using his vast knowledge to help and heal others.

The more I learned, the more I wanted to learn. I wanted to know how every organ, cell, vessel, and membrane functioned. When you understand the body, you will come to realize that people don't suffer from headaches because their bodies aren't producing enough aspirin; nor do they have high blood pressure because their bodies are lacking water pills or any of the other blood pressure medications.

When God created us, He also developed a plan for us to follow in our everyday diets. That plan was published in the Bible. For your convenience, it's right up front in Genesis [1:29], the very first book of the Bible, and it's in the very first paragraph, so you don't have to go digging. And for those of you who don't even want to do that much, I'll tell you what it says: "And God said, 'Behold, I have given you every plant yielding seed that is on the face of all the Earth, and every tree with seed in its fruit. You shall have them for food.'" That is what he planned for us to eat. So think about it; have you ever seen a doughnut tree? How about a steak or potato chip tree? A candy bush maybe? Maybe these items weren't meant to be our food. Think about it. If we were meant to consume garbage, we wouldn't need garbage cans. By the way, speaking of every tree with seed in its fruit, there's a certain manufacturer who has produced crops that don't have seeds.

After that first fast, I adopted a diet that included nothing but raw foods. The only cooking that was done in my household was Mother Nature's cooking. You may have read the book I wrote by that title. I also began to participate in some fasts, compliments of various states. The first was in Washington State, in the summer of 1968. I had joined the Nisqually Indians in a demonstration, and as a result served forty-five days in the Olympia, Washington, state prison. I fasted for forty-five days. Every year for the next four years, the summer would find me in another state, locked up for another reason, and being treated to another fasting period. The hunger I experienced during those fasts caused me to do a lot of thinking. I thought about all the times I went to bed hungry. I also thought about the hungry, starving people all over the world and wondered what if there was one nutrient that could be used to feed hungry people throughout the planet? I stopped wondering and got to work developing a formula, with the help of some scientists, nutritionists, and health experts, to deal with world hunger. I had learned enough about the power of herbs, vitamins, and juices that I knew somewhere, somehow there was just the right combination of these ingredients that would not only boost a person's immune system, but also help them gain more energy. I had read a lot about kelp and heard that it was considered an ideal source of renewable energy. Kelp is actually the catchall name for a variety of large brown seaweeds, abundantly available off the coast of Japan and along the west coast of the United States. There is government documentation affirming the fact that oil extracted from seaweed contained one thousand times more vitamins A and D than an equal quantity of cod liver oil.

I spent the next couple of years creating a superfood, with kelp as the base. I gave this formula the name Formula 4X because, among its many other attributes, it was four times as potent as any other nutritional supplement. I knew this instinctively because of the ingredients that were in it and their proportions. I wanted to know for sure, so I put it to the ultimate test.

I was planning a thousand-mile cross-country run, from Chicago to Washington, DC, to dramatize world and domestic hunger. I wasn't going to eat anything during that run—no solid food. I decided that I would run fifty-one miles a day for seven days, taking nothing but a little of the formula I put together, and some fruit juice. I was not only protesting world hunger, but I wanted to prove that the world doesn't need food; it needs nutrition.

I made it to Washington, DC, and ran up the Capitol steps in August 1974. Two years later, I planned another run to protest world hunger. This time I decided to run from Los Angeles to New York. I left Los Angeles on April 22, 1976, running only on water, juice, and my 4X Formula. A couple of people joined me. Most of them lasted a couple of miles. Muhammad Ali lasted the longest but gave up after awhile. Later on, he wrote a poem for me, in typical Ali fashion:

Dick Gregory has speed
Dick Gregory has endurance
But if you're going to run with him
Increase your insurance.

As a matter of fact, Ali used my 4X Formula during the time he was in training for his fight with Ken Norton. He beat Norton and credited 4X Formula with helping him win.

I arrived in New York on July 4, 1976. Some folks think they can't last on a three-day fast when they're sitting around, doing nothing. This was the first of many nutritional formulations that I developed. Another was called Correction Connection, formulated to help people on drugs kick the habit. I put the 4X Formula in an Ethiopian hospital, and children that would have been dead in eighteen months walked out of that hospital, very much alive!

Word of mouth spread quickly. People were talking about how they gained energy and lost weight with 4X Formula and how they kicked the drug habit with the Correction Connection. My phone was ringing off the hook. John Lennon, Marvin Gaye, and Randy Jackson of the Jackson Five were among my famous clients. Perhaps Randy's one of the most remarkable cases because when Joe Jackson called me in 1980 after Randy had been in a terrible accident, the doctors were hours away from amputating his right leg. We immediately started treating him with 4X Formula. *JET* magazine ran a story about his remarkable recovery several months later, and Randy was quoted as saying, "I was taking this formula Dick Gregory had given me . . . and the doctors couldn't believe how strong my bones are now."

I had a chance to try out the formula again when I fasted for the release of the Iranian hostages. That fast lasted three weeks. I lost twenty-five pounds, but thanks to 4X Formula, I maintained an abundance of energy.

I noticed that the starving Ethiopians had bald heads and big stomachs. Then I noticed that well-fed businessmen also had bald heads and big stomachs. That taught me that malnutrition has two ends—one from not getting enough nutrition; and the other from getting poor nutrition that was malfunctioning.

So I took the formula, which I originally put together to increase strength and stamina, and changed it to a weight-loss formula. I thought about changing the name but decided that 4X was still the best name.

My partner, John Bellamy, and I created a mail-order company and mapped out a strategy through which we could get the product to people through our company. In Chicago, John developed an ingenious marketing plan for distributing a newly formulated weight-loss product called Dick Gregory's Slim-Safe Bahamian Diet. 4X Formula was the basis for this product, which helped thousands of people successfully lose weight. We also opened the Dick Gregory International Health Institute in Nassau in 1985. Many obese people who came to the Institute thought their situation was impossible. To them, we were miracle workers. *Ebony* magazine did a story about a young boy who we had helped to lose weight and gain a life. A young man from Brooklyn, New York, by the name of Ron High read that story and came to us, hoping we could help him shed the majority of his 850-pound girth. We had to use a freight scale from Delta Air Lines at La Guardia Airport to get his weight, because a regular scale only goes up to seven hundred pounds.

Today, there's a reality TV show called *The Biggest Loser*. That's what we were doing before reality TV even existed, only our clients weren't losers—they were winners. If I ever have a reality show about weight loss, I'll call it *The Biggest Winners*. In order to reach Americans, you have to do it with glamour. I want to glamorize health and nutrition the same way we have glamorized athletics and sports. We have got to make health an issue in America. We have to make teenagers just as excited about drinking fresh juice as they are about buying a pair of Michael Jordan's tennis shoes.

If you go into any health store today, you will see shelves and shelves of powdered meal-replacement mixes that promise weight loss. My Slim-Safe Bahamian Diet could replace a meal, or several meals, but it is much more than a meal-replacement drink mix. Not only does it have all of the vitamins and herbs to sustain a person, but when we reformulated it, we added even more metabolism-building and fat-burning ingredients. Kelp was one of the original ingredients and continued to play a huge role in making Slim-Safe Bahamian Diet a miracle weight-loss product.

When obesity visits your body, it doesn't come by itself. It brings along its partners in crime: migraine headaches, bad sinuses, muscle and joint aches and pains, gout, arthritis, diabetes, kidney disease, high blood pressure, and a bunch of allergies. When you lose weight through a plan that focuses on natural, nutritious eating and exercise, all of obesity's "cousins" will leave along with the unwanted fat.

AMANDLA FESTIVAL, HARVARD STADIUM, BOSTON

(July 21, 1979)

The list of causes championed by Dick Gregory continued to grow throughout the 1970s: free speech, the anti-nuclear movement, women's rights, Native American rights, human rights. He felt keenly drawn to the liberation movement in South Africa, and in 1979 he spoke at the Amandla Festival, a concert headlined by Bob Marley and a rally against inequality in South Africa and in the US.

Let me say to all of you that's here for this fantastic, beautiful occasion, let me personally say thanks to you, to each and every one of you. And I can't tell you how good I feel as I stand here and look at you out there, and I just hope that when you leave here, you won't leave here just on an entertainment high, but you will leave here and take what this affair is about today. Because none of us on the stage have to look for another place to entertain, but we go out of our way to find people that want to come together, to talk about unity, to talk about love, to talk about peace, to talk about respect for one another as human beings. That's what this is all about today, and that's what you're here for, and that's what you are part of. And I say when you leave here, take it with you, and that's what's going to turn the world around. A sick, insane, degenerate political network around the world that's manipulated by a handful of evil, sick, slimy, degenerate men will never be any good. But there's nothing on this planet Earth that you can invent—like a gun, or missile, or atomic energy—that scares them, because they can deal with all of it. The one thing they cannot deal with is what you're doing here today. There's not a Pentagon on this planet that can stop what we are about today, because when we talk about unity, and talk about love, and talk about peace, and talk about respect, that transcends all the things that evil people can put together. That's what it's about. South Africa to you should start right here within your own self. First, we got to admit that we're racist. First, we got to admit that we sexist. First we got to admit that we don't give a damn about poor people, and sick people, and minority people. Once we start admitting that, then we can start changing. It's a beautiful thing for us to look to our brothers and sisters in South Africa and say we care about you. But don't forget these Indian brothers and sisters in America, who we stole this damn country from. We must care about them too. You see, it is so easy to love people that's a long ways away from us. But can you love yourself? Can you go back home from that house you left that wasn't unified today, and can this affair have enough effect on you to make you go back home to your apartment, to your house, to your area, and work for unity? That's what it's all about. That's what it's all about, because if we cannot have unity here, it's a poor unity we're going to get for our brothers and sisters in South Africa. All over the world I think about those people that's out in the water today, and I look at the names we're calling them: "boat people." They're not boat people; they're people that's about to die, and we the decent people on this planet must stand up and say to the rest of them inhumane, cruel beasts that we are not going to tolerate it no more. And then they'll say, "What you gonna do about it?" If I don't do nothing but get out of my bed every day, and look myself in the face in the quietness of my living room, and say, "I'm not going to tolerate it no more," that alone—when enough people start doing it—is enough to win. I say to you that we can turn this around. And I say to you that when you leave here, feel good knowing that we're saying to the whole world that help is on the way. That we are concerned about you. And I say to all of these entertainers that gave up their time to be here, it's about more than just entertaining you. When we come and see what you're doing, you do something for us, and I thank you.

I wish I could stand here today and tell you that the number one problem in this country is racism, the number one problem is sexism. I wish I could tell you the number one problem is the gap between the rich and the poor. I wish I could tell you that the number one problem is hunger. Those are all problems, but if those were the problems, we could solve them overnight. The main problem is not racism and sexism and all of that craziness. The number one problem is not the nuclear plants. The number one problem is America is morally and spiritually bankrupt. That's what the problem is. And it is our job to say to America—in no uncertain terms— that we're going to turn this country around. And what goes on over there in South Africa, there's no other group or nation on this planet that's more responsible for that condition than the United States of America.

IRAN HOSTAGE CRISIS: PRESS CONFERENCE AT LOGAN AIRPORT, BOSTON

(September 9, 1980)

In November 1979, supporters of the new Iranian leader Ayatollah Khomeini seized sixty-six Americans at the US embassy in Tehran. They were held hostage in an attempt to force the return to Iran of Mohammad Reza Shah Pahlavi, the recently toppled Iranian ruler whom the CIA had helped seize power in 1953. Six months into the crisis, Dick Gregory went to Iran to fast and pray for the release of the hostages. While there, the ayatollah asked to speak with him. Gregory met with Khomeini, refusing to act as a representative of the US government, but hoping to move the impasse beyond the realm of politics. The following are his comments at a press conference upon his return to the US in September 1980.

I don't know how long I'll sit in front of the White House, but that's the next thing that I have planned. I would hope that this condition [the Iranian hostage crisis] would be relieved. I think it is ripe to be relieved. I think that if anybody thinks it can be solved now without making political concessions . . . Let me just say this: regardless of what is thought about the Iranian government and the

Iranian people, they're into prayers. That's why they love me. They are *into* prayers. I would suggest that anybody dealing with them should read the Koran.

The Koran talks about forgiveness, talks about pardoning people only after you have admitted it, and I think that's very important. It is a violation against their religion to pardon or to show mercy without you first saying, "I did it, and I'm sorry." So knowing the politics—and I don't know if Jimmy Carter could do that now—I would suggest that some religious leaders be sent there very soon to look at that situation and decide if America should apologize. Then Jimmy Carter's off the hook politically.

Repenting, that's what our whole religious structure is about. I would apologize for what has gone on in that country down through the years, the CIA's involvement, the amount of money that was spent in that country on military equipment. There's military equipment I think we should buy back, because Iran has never been able to use it. The Russians have offered to buy it, and Iran won't sell it to them. Out of all the crazy things you hear them say about us, it's like a picnic compared to what they say about Russia.

But they see our [lack of] integrity. The CIA in Iran is funding the rebels in Afghanistan. Iran has told the world we're giving them guns. America said we're not, and they know we are. They see living examples of it. I think Jimmy Carter and the military might have a problem with it now.

I'll tell you this: we jump on weak folks. We never attacked a Russian in this country when they were financing the North Vietnamese to kill Americans, and if Russia signed a defense pact with Iran in the morning, we'd have a different attitude. There's a lot of things that go on with that country because they're weak. We have to understand their strategic position, and if we force them, they will back into that Russian camp, and then we've really got some problems.

Had this government listened to Malcolm X, they would have heard Khomeini. Had they listened to Stokely and Rap and the SNCC youngsters, they would have heard the revolutionary students. They were saying the same thing.

PILGRIM IN SEARCH OF LIBERATION: *MESSAGE* MAGAZINE

(March/April 1981)

Twenty years ago, Dick Gregory was a stand-up comic on the nightclub circuit. By his own account he smoked and drank heavily. Gregory had an eye that saw through the games people and institutions play. He had a wit that broke up huge audiences while making them see truths about themselves. But that eye and that wit were teamed with a heart that was being led to the more important issues of life. Gregory's priorities shifted. His concerns became oppression, manipulation, racism, and war. He discovered that the body is the temple of the Holy Spirit and is not to be defiled. He became a prophet to the secular world about the evils of bodily abuse, particularly through diet. When Gregory yells "Foul!" about an oppressive institution or agency or group of people or lifestyle, he doesn't make a case like a lawyer with a long list of proofs. No, Gregory thinks analogically. He looks for parallels. He's not hung up trying to prove cause and effect. If a window breaks each time a guy waves his arm, Gregory doesn't have to see him throw the stone. But enough—Gregory can speak for himself.

MESSAGE: You say research indicating that the typical American diet has many harmful elements in it that has not been made readily available to the masses. Instead, the interests of the rich and powerful are protected at almost any cost to the poor and the powerless. What does all this have to do with diet? And can you give us examples of manipulation of the masses?

GREGORY: You know, I do think much of the salvation of the planet is in diet. Another thing is how easy it is to get into it. You don't have to change all of your eating habits. Here's a little thing: just add bran to your diet in the morning and in the evening, and you can cancel out about 80 percent of the diseases in the lower digestive tract. And you know the way they got into that?

They got into Africa. They happened to meet this group of Africans whose systems were regular. They began checking, and they found out that within twenty-four hours, everything they had eaten had passed completely through their systems. From there it led to the roughage theory. This was already suspected, but for follow-up, researchers found some of this same group of Africans who had moved to Western society. This group was winding up with the same kinds of diseases as people in the West. So when you cook string beans and take the strings off, your roughage is gone. The lesson for us: add some bran.

I usually tell people to go to a health food store and get the pure bran. But it's different in dealing with the masses, you know, because the minute you say, "Go to the health food store," it turns them off. "You mean you're asking me to change my diet, and then what I've got to find is hidden somewhere? Plus, you know, I'm not all that upset about the way I'm eating. I'm just trying this change out of respect and knowing where you're coming from." So I tell them to get bran or whole wheat cereal. Now I hate to send people to that commercial scene, but bran is bran. Some commercial preparations have sugar, but I'm saying that once they start on it, in about a two-week period, eating a bowl in the morning and a bowl in the evening will have a fantastic effect. I say eat a bowl of bran because people are not likely to believe it would only take a teaspoonful. They can't see a teaspoon doing nothing. They'd just say, "Later for the whole idea. I'll just forget about it."

MESSAGE: How did you start informing yourself on health issues?

GREGORY: I used to go to health food stores at first, or other places. I bought six or seven hundred dollars' worth of books. I have researchers on my staff, and I use Harvard's library. I also used my own common sense. I started asking myself, "If dead animals' flesh is so good for you, why don't cows eat it? If protein is so necessary in that form, why don't the animals need it?" I began to realize you don't have to eat hair to grow hair; you don't have to eat fingernails to grow fingernails. If you put the right minerals and things into your body, it will manufacture what you need. That's the wonder of this body. When I was eating meat, the most I weighed was 134, but when I started a vegetarian diet, I went to 288. This was from ignorance. I thought I needed a substitute, and that substitute was eating five or six times a day. But then I learned about fasting. In 1967 I went on my first forty-day fast, and I went from 288 to 95 pounds. My energy level was incredible, just so high!

Then I learned you must pray while fasting, and during my second fast, prayer made a difference. I've been trying to get people to fast from sundown Friday to sundown Saturday, and use that time to meditate and to pray that hungry people will be fed. But the important thing is the government. They act as if they don't have the research. The former Department of Health, Education, and Welfare was really pushed with questions on why we don't have serious research on vegetarianism. They said, "The only thing we have ever studied was from England." But they have piles of it [research on vegetarianism]. There are piles of documents concerning what they have studied about your group [Seventh-day Adventists].

MESSAGE: In a sense, you're saying the government is not making available the information it has. Is this what you mean by governmental manipulation and control?

GREGORY: We live in a country today that can ship tanks all the way around the world but cannot ship turnips to starving people. We have no business living on a planet where people are dying from starvation. There are enough folks with enough know-how to feed everybody. We are all born with certain God-given rights to drink [clean] water, the right to breathe [fresh] air, and the right to eat. And we've got to let people know that we are not dealing with any more trickery.

MESSAGE: Trickery?

GREGORY: Yes! Look at this Iran thing. The day I left Iran I bought this soft drink mix right in Iran. The boycott was in Iran, yet I bought these grits—the same grits the president [former President Jimmy Carter] ate in the White House. I bought this Vaseline in Iran. Anything available in Iran before the boycott, I could still buy months later, and yet high anti-Iranian sentiment was developing even then. The Iranian people couldn't understand it. They couldn't understand how we were all so upset over the hostages' being taken that we were jumping at everything Iranian, when they could go to the supermarket and find every American product they were ever able to find. It still must be emphasized that no one in his right mind—and no sane, honest people—could ever justify taking hostages, under any circumstances. But there are some circumstances. We need to know what led up to the hostage-taking so we can work to do the things in other countries that will prevent what happened in Iran. Look at this FBI thing, this Abscam. Eight congressmen and one senator. We should rise up and say, "Hey, how did you all choose them? What criteria did you use to pick all of them? And why has no one in the major press done a serious research job to find out what relationship these officials have with the FBI?"

Persistent rumors linking the CIA with the People's Temple in Jonestown has been the subject of congressional investigation, and I think we should really be concerned about the CIA, Jonestown, and mind-control drugs being tested. Because the next thing you know, they might be showing up in your hamburgers; they might be showing up in your breakfast cereal, and the next thing you know . . . How are nine hundred people all going to commit suicide and neatly lie face down after drinking cyanide? There's nothing on the planet that creates spasms and convulsions like cyanide. Then we were told that the dogs and the cats and the pets drank the grape too. You can't get a dog, even the dumbest dog you can find, to drink with anything in it, let alone cyanide—and there are some dumb dogs.

Then there's that Pinto! You know, they told Ford Motor Company that these gasoline tanks in the back were dangerous. If they were bumped from the rear the gas tank would explode, and with $14 we can correct that. They said, "Wait a minute, let's figure that up—$14 times . . . that will be $58 million! Roll them like they are because whatever lawsuit we get won't cost us $58 million." Did you know that? It came out in a trial. And Ford Motor Company is still permitted to do business as usual. Not one person in Ford Motor Company has gone to jail. But I'll bet if it had been some Black company, ain't gonna mess with nobody with no power that might mess with you back. That's what the whole ball game is about. We all have got a big stake in this thing—in making this country, this planet, work right—because we've got no place to go; we're stuck with this one. But don't believe that a handful of crazies are going to tear this planet up. The same God that put this planet here will be the same God that will tear it up whenever He decides to tear it up, and that God does not need any of us to help Him do it.

MESSAGE: Seventh-day Adventists have been advocates of healthful living with attention called to the vegetarian diet since our early days. We're interested in reaching the man on the street. What are your suggestions?

GREGORY: You have to exhibit it, and you have to leave leeway. It's very important to leave leeway for the horror of coming through grade school, high school, and college. Mothers and fathers—you know, the people that love us—never told us that meat was bad. It's very difficult for a stranger to tell us, when we're believing all the teachings of the people that love us. If you go around to a Black person's house, and you don't eat meat, they feel sorry for you. I mean, when I first turned vegetarian, it seemed to attract women. Women just wanted to be with me because they felt sorry for me. You know, "Oh, my soul, you don't eat meat?" If you'd go to their houses, they'd pile your plate up. It was just the most incredible thing in the world. They never looked at it as a strength. Mothers are the same way. And then you get grandmothers trying to slip stuff to your children. The same things happened to ours. I had started out with the candy. The kids were off candy. We would come into the house, and we wouldn't accept candy and cookies. "Zero my soul," folks would say, "Gregory is so mean." But I think what has to happen is that we document on a very unsophisticated level that we don't have to eat it. I think my next book will deal with the spiritual side of things.

Your material would need to go out on two levels. Write a column for the adult and then write a column for the child—something like coloring a page or a coloring book. The important thing is to get them introduced to what a carrot is. . . . You see, out of all the ways to commit suicide, even brutal ones, no one's gonna drink iodine because of the skull and crossbones. You've seen it as a child. That's the level you have to work on. I tell you what would be interesting in your church, a study on the sexual temperament. That's where Gandhi really got into his movements, you know. He was trying to cut back his sexual urge and control his diet. I just wonder what it's like for people who go without all the toxins in the body.

What is the strength of the family, and what is the temperament of the church, of your church? Are you losing? Are you having problems?

MESSAGE: What is your advice to our readers, mostly Black people in America?

GREGORY: Decide! Decide you're going to have some integrity about your body. Decide you're not going to put any soda pop, or beer, or reefers, or booze, or cocaine—none of that craziness—in your body. And see how good you feel. You may decide you want to feel that way all day. I've gone the whole route. I've been up to 288 pounds, smoked four packs of cigarettes a day, and drunk a fifth of Scotch every day, and I can tell you there's nothing in it. You're playing a game on yourself. If you see the way we disrespect our bodies, then you can see why the people who manipulate us can get by with what they can get by with. I beg you to please, please, start checking out your food.

Some run around saying, "I'm into soul food, baby. Whitey can't cook." Whitey don't want no soul food! Anybody can cook that old grease that we be cooking! But do you realize two out of every three Black folks in this country have a serious problem with high blood pressure, sugar diabetes, hypertension; and we're sitting there eating all that old crazy stuff saying, "Yeah, man, I bet white folk can't eat like this." Any old fool can cook cornbread. White folk raised the hogs and the chickens, and you expect they can't cook them if they wanted to? Anybody can cook a chicken. A chicken can cook itself!

When you go to the store, just play a game with yourself. Read the ingredients, and you'll see five or six words you can't even pronounce. Why eat it? What I'm about to do now is go twelve years with no sex, no talking, no eating solid food. I'm going the whole route to dramatize my protest against racism, against wars, and to gain moral power. I am calling for no war ever! If your son is six years old, and my son is seven years old, when I come off of this thing they'll be eighteen or nineteen. At first, people will laugh, but then every time they think about sex, they'll think about me and this whole thing. There'll be joking and laughing, "Ha, ha, ha." But then the jokes will stop.

"SOMETHING MUST BE WRONG": ADDRESS AT THE CLEVELAND CITY CLUB

(March 18, 1983)

EMCEE: Good afternoon. Welcome to the City Club Forum. Today, our speaker is Dick Gregory, a person well known to us for so many reasons. He gained fame originally as a comedian. But he is, today, a variety of things: human rights activist, social satirist, author, lecturer, recording artist, actor, philosopher, political activist. He seeks to combine these roles to serve the cause of human liberation and to alleviate human suffering. Mr. Gregory used comedy as an expedient avenue to gain people's attention, to make them think as well as to laugh. His success as a comedian enabled him to assist causes he believed were in need of help. You know him well for his participation in the civil rights movement of the 1960s, his efforts toward world peace, the alleviation of hunger, and the rights of American Indians.

For a time, he was virtually barred from the entertainment business, and he has been jailed on various occasions for his participation in demonstrations. In 1974, Mr. Gregory ran from Chicago to Washington, DC, to call attention to world hunger. Since then, he has employed fasts to symbolize the suffering of oppressed people. In 1980, he journeyed to Iran, and over a period of 145 days, he took only liquids as he prayed for the release of the American hostages and the end to the hostilities. While in Iran, he was the last westerner to meet with the Ayatollah Khomeini. In 1982, he counseled hunger strikers in Illinois to aid those working for passage of the Equal Rights Amendment. A self-taught authority on nutrition, Mr. Gregory is the author of nine books, which include some on the subject of nutrition, in addition to the best-known, his autobiographical book, *Nigger*. It's clear that Mr. Gregory is a difficult man to label. He asks that he be described today as a man with a voice for people. It gives me great pleasure to introduce a man for people, Dick Gregory.

Let me say thank you very much and God bless you. Let me say first that I thank and praise God that you and I made it here safely today, and I pray to God that your return and my return will be equally as safe. Let me first say thanks to the City Club that has had this forum since 1912. I think that we join various groups and clubs for different reasons, but I think what you do here can be very important. If I was the president of the United States right this moment, I would come here personally and let the whole world know how I feel about a forum like this. Of course, I would study it before I get committed to see what y'all have really been doing, but the potential is there.

I'm not the president, so the first thing I did when I got here was check all the exits out. If something happens and you're an audience, sometimes your whole thought pattern leaves you. You sit there and say, "I smell something like smoke." I beg you to understand, there's nothing like smoke that's not smoke. If you're ever sitting at a public gathering and you smell something like smoke, just take my word for it, it is. When I go in a hotel—and I'm in ho-tels almost every night for ten months—the first thing I do is put my bags down and go check the exits out. Then I walk from the exit to my room with my eyes closed. It's very embarrassing in hotels. Sometimes they put money in your hand. Sometimes you find a couple of keys in your hand. Ninety-eight percent of the people in this country that die in fires die in homes, and that's kind of weird, because it's one of the few places in America where we don't have fire drills.

I hope if anyone that's in this building now in a wheelchair or is handicapped, I hope you've got enough sense to sit right next to the exit. Because if anything happens, probably everybody will run off and leave you. As a matter of fact, if I was in a wheelchair, knowing the way we treat handicapped folks in this country, I wouldn't only sit next to the door with my wheelchair, if anything happened, I would jump and leave the chair to block the rest of y'all. Then after it was guaranteed I was the only survivor, I would say to the press, "I stayed with them as long as I could. You know, they just won't follow a cripple."

I wonder what day in this country will we treat handicapped folks with dignity and respect. And I'm guilty; I parked in the handicapped parking twice. I don't do it anymore, but I have. The first time wasn't my fault. Now they have these little handicapped medallions, blue with a white stick figure so when you see that, you know. They haven't always had that. It just used to be a sign that said, "Handicapped Parking." And I really thought that was for us, so I jumped out of my car and said, "'Bout time!" Another time I was really guilty. I was in this shopping center looking for a place to park, and I was really in a hurry. It wasn't going to take long; I just had to run into the washroom. I didn't see a parking space and

I was really having a lot of pressure, so I parked in the handicapped parking, ran in, and I was still zipping up my pants when I came out. Twelve white cats in wheelchairs had surrounded my car. With an attitude. So naturally I said, "What's going on, guys?" They said, "Some Black dude done parked in our parking space. We're going to deal with him when he comes back!" It was obvious they didn't know it was me. I said, "I just can't believe that some Black cat can be that insensitive to crippled white boys. Let me deal with him for you!" This one white guy was really touched. He started crying and said, "You mean you are willing to do in another Black, for us?" I said, "Oh man, that happens all the time." He said, "What are you going to do?" I said, "I'm gonna steal the nigger's car!"

I wonder what day will we in this country learn to treat the handicapped? That's just the beginning. It keeps on, and on, and on, and on. It's kind of interesting. When I look at the number one movie—E.T.—I don't believe this ugly, strange-looking, weird . . . People say, "Well, I love it!" Then I realize how certain people have manipulated our heads. We can make them love it, as long as it doesn't look like another person. We can make them wear it on their T-shirts and bring it home in the form of dolls as long as it doesn't look like a Jew. As long as it doesn't look like an Indian, a Chicano, a Puerto Rican, or an Asian American. As long as it doesn't look like a mother. As long as you can reduce it down to some ugly, insignificant nothing, we will love it. I don't understand that. When was the last time you wore your mother on a T-shirt? When was the last time we put elderly people, that go to bed every night worried, scared, and hungry while we, the mightiest, richest, wealthiest nation in the world . . . As long as that doesn't look like another person. That's kind of sad.

And yet I say to you today we've matured. America is much

more mature today than it was before the days of the civil rights movement, the '60s, Martin Luther King, Malcolm X. Somewhere I keep hearing Black folks and white folks trying to apologize for that era. [People say,] "Martin Luther King was a communist . . ." I wonder why we live in a system where everything good that happens to me, the communists get blamed for it, but they ain't never blamed all them niggers that are selling dope as being communist-inspired. I ain't never heard that Black prostitute, and all those thugs and pimps that run through my neighborhood, I have never heard anybody say that Russia is behind them. [*laughter*] But the minute I walk through with the dignity and respect that the Constitution tells me I'm supposed to have, there's supposed to be some secret plot.

I listen to white folks: some of them complain about us, and you wouldn't believe, listening to them, that we were kidnapped. I mean, you'd think we came over here on a fourteen-day visa! I was listening to a radio show the other night: "Them coloreds can't even talk English!" They were talking about this new college test. That ain't nothing but a game. I as a Black father with ten Black children that have gone through grade school, high school, and college, they know what the whole game is about. That test everybody's got to take to go to college—they didn't have that test in the early '40s. That test was put together to protect the integrity of Ivy League schools, when certain white folks were getting some money to go. That test doesn't have anything to do with my intelligence, because I can give white folks the greatest Shakespearean test you ever had, written up in Black lingo, and you'd flunk it. That whole game. "I like Harold Washington, but it's Jesse Jackson that . . ."

I'm tired of hearing white folks talk about Jesse. I don't hear y'all talk about the Mafia. The Mafia reduced a whole generation of children in this country to drugs, and nobody wants to deal with it. And you call yourself free. That's why forums like this are important. A free, democratic society that talks about freedom of speech has to be that. But most Americans are afraid. We don't want to talk about that 6 percent of the population that controls 90 percent of the wealth yet pays less than 19 percent of the income tax, because when you get to messing with them, they'll blow your whole block up. We don't want to talk about a system where the whole planet Earth, right this moment as we sit here, every minute you sit here today, forty-one people die from starvation. Now what bothers me about that is when I turn on the TV, and I see white farmers punching a white sheriff in the nose because their farm is about to be repossessed, and nobody wants to deal with the fact forty-one people can die every minute because there's not enough to eat, and farmers are talking about being repossessed. Something don't jive. Something doesn't make sense. A planet where billions of people are hungry and farmers in America are leaving the farm, coming to the large urban cities, standing in the unemployment line? Something's wrong.

Something's wrong when the mightiest, Christian, religious nation in the world continually cries over the crucifixion of Christ but doesn't get rid of capital punishment. I can't believe that we Christians can be that ignorant, not to know that Christ died because the state had capital punishment. If Jesus Christ came back to America today and bugged the same people, they'd give him the electric chair. Then all of y'all would be walking around with big chairs around your neck.

How long? One day maybe we'll take it back and find out that we're

getting so wild now because of what we eat. You look at television—
I wouldn't permit one of them in my house with my ten children—
y'all go home and look at television and tell me when is the last time
you saw a carrot on TV. When is the last time you saw a peach on
TV? Something's wrong.

I picked up the paper today. This is the biggest headline going
now, right down from where I live, New Bedford. Six dudes just got
indicted for raping a woman, while the others stood and cheered
it on. Everybody said, "Didn't anyone call somebody? Didn't anybody help?" And then the same day, another paper has a headline,
"Whistle Blower Ousted in the Defense Department." Here's a cat
that blew the whistle on folks stealing money in the Defense Department, and he loses his job! Everybody's complaining that no
one wants to talk in America, but if you talk on the wrong people
in America, they will kill you. And you know that. So why do we
play all these games? It's okay to talk on some purse snatcher, but
walk up here one day and call the name of the head of the Mafia in
this town, talk about them, and see what happens to you. Try it.
A newspaper in Phoenix, Arizona, was doing a Mafia story, and a
guy got in his car and the whole car blew up. Killed him. Newspaper reporters came in from all over the world, and when they got
through doing the report, it not only led into the major politicians
in the state, but to the folks that owned the newspaper. And that
newspaper refused to write the report. The only reason the people
of Phoenix got it was because a paper came in from out of town.

I got a president that goes to South America and gives some
hoodlum, thug generals $2 billion of our tax money, and nobody
raised their voice. But our elderly people, whose old age pension
check is running out before the end of the month, you ask for some
money, and they look at you like you're crazy. Astronauts just went

up and they couldn't perform their experiments because their suits didn't work. Two suits that cost $300 million. Now y'all have bought enough outfits to know . . . no outfit costs that much. But we have two of them. Three hundred million dollars. They didn't work, and to this day nobody's been indicted. But our elderly people, who have proved they will work, nobody's concerned about giving them $300 million to see to it that the ends can meet. Something's wrong.

Oh, I read the paper every day. All of them. "Twenty Million Dollar Ruling Against Ford Motor Company Cited." "Ford Motor Company is paying about $20 million as a result of lawsuits charging that defective automobile and truck transmissions caused scores of deaths and injuries." Then it goes on to say that it could have been corrected for 3 cents per vehicle. There would have to be pure hate that one human being has for another human being that wouldn't correct something that's going to kill you, and when it costs 3 cents, and the cost is going to be passed on to you for $300. I think when you see these headlines, you see what we have to change in America. Twenty million dollars in rulings against Ford Motor Company, and in the same day, the headline in the *Chicago Tribune*, "Three Cents Repair Job Might Have Saved Ford $20 Million in Lawsuits." The day you know we're making this a great nation is when you read, "Three Cents Repair Job Might Have Saved X Amount of Lives," not $20 million.

We've got an educational system that's so busy teaching you how to make a living, they don't even pretend to care about how you live. And it works because it feeds into the greed machine. "Oh I know cigarette smoking causes cancer, but I can't stop smoking. . . ." I ain't got no problem with you smokers. What bothers me, had those same scientists told you smoking cigarettes in your automobile would corrode your engine, there would be no more smoking in the car. That frightens me. I can sympathize with cigarette smokers because I used to smoke four packs a day. If I was still smoking, I would lead the rally that they charge us 10 cents more a pack, for an insurance policy. So when those cigarettes wipe us out, our family, friends, loved ones, and the United States government are covered—to the tune of $27 billion every year that taxpayers pay because of the injuries and death caused by cigarettes.

When will we change it? When we start having respect for our bodies, and a little less respect for money. The number two cause of cancer today is salt. The number three killer on planet Earth is white refined sugar. And they keep us so ignorant that parents give it to their children as a reward called candy. Something's wrong.

Oh, we talk about the violence in America, the public schools that are out of hand. Why don't you press people do some research? You'll find out that the violence, and heavy dumbness in public schools, started the same year the school lunch program started. It's the chemicals, and the additives, and the poisons that they put in the food. Half the children when they finish eating want to burn the building down; the other half want to go to sleep.

There's something wrong with a nation where the top four killers of young folks . . . Number one is automobile accidents, drunk driving. They're not buying the whiskey; it's in the house. The number two killer is homicide. They're not buying the guns; we've got the guns. The number one mightiest Christian society in the world, we've got a Bible and a gun, and we're too out of it to know that houses where guns are, God is not, because God and guns can't occupy the same spot. The number three killer of young folks: cancer. The number four killer of young folks in America: suicide. And the fifth killer is drugs. If I came down here from another planet, and they told me about this nation and how great it is and how mighty it is, all I'd have to do is look at that list of what's killing your young folks and know something's wrong.

And it's already out there. They don't teach it at Harvard, Yale, and Case Western. But it's here. [holds up newspaper] "Diet and delinquency have been tied in." The government has done one of the most fantastic studies at the Tidewater Detention Center, where they know that 98 percent of your hardened, repeat violent criminals eat a minimum of 450 pounds of white sugar a year, while the average American eats 128 pounds. They did a blind study, took half the children off white refined sugar and left the other half on, then sent a team of doctors in there and didn't tell what was what. Every one of them that wasn't eating sugar, you could see a total disappearance of violence and hostility. How can you go through grade school, high school, and college—taught how to make money, but not how to live—without asking some questions?

Today, a fine article in one of the better papers in the world, *USA Today*. They've got an article in today's paper, you should read it. It's another one of these things we're scared to talk about in America, one of our problems that has reached epidemic proportions. But we don't want to talk about our problems in a free democratic society. We're one of the few countries in the world that can wipe out venereal disease, but the only country in the world where venereal disease is running rampant because nobody wants to talk about it. "The new skeleton in our closets: parents are getting beat up by their children." As you read the article, most of them are boys beating up their mama. Don't nobody want to talk about it because it's so embarrassing; we don't want to get no help. But if we trace it back to the diet, we might find out why. So somewhere, we're going to have to start dealing with what we eat.

Dr. Ben Feingold's book *Why Your Child Is Hyper-active*—he took a bunch of slow-learning, dumb, backwards children in Palo Alto, California, that were told they couldn't even come to school. He didn't even give them good food. All he did was take the chemicals and additives out of their food, and within six months' time, they were back in school and had reached their grade level. There's more stomach cancer caused every day from drinking coffee than lung cancer from smoking cigarettes. While the old folks want to run around and talk about, "I wonder what these youngsters are doing on drugs," the number one drugs in this country are nicotine and caffeine. If you don't believe it, hide your coffee tonight. And cold turkey it in the morning. But we like what we like, and everybody's got somebody they put down. The whiskey drinkers ain't never liked the winos. Reefer smokers now think they're more sophisticated than whiskey drinkers. Cocaine snorters think they're hipper than reefer smokers, and coffee drinkers hate them all.

I say to you today we can make that difference. There's no need in a nation this mighty and this strong, spending the billions of dollars we spend for heart conditions, and high blood pressure, and sugar diabetes. We've got the finest machines in the world, but what about people? The mightiest nation is not the nation with the biggest bomb or the biggest army or the mightiest fleet. The mightiest nation in the world is the nation that has the healthiest people, mentally and physically. You can play games with that if you want, but you better play them quick and you better play them fast because recess is just about over.

Somewhere we can make that difference. Somewhere you can determine your health. Somewhere we've got to ask questions. If chlorine and fluoride in my water is good for me, how come you rich folks don't drink it? Every time I come around y'all, you're getting yours out of a bottle, and it ain't got no chlorine and fluoride in it. I've got enough sense to know if it was good for me, I wouldn't get it for free. I've got enough sense to also know that every time I get ready to put water in with my goldfish, it says if you take the water out of the tap (with chlorine and fluoride in it), let it sit open in a container for twenty-four hours or you'll kill the fish. It looks like somebody is saying, "Now, what is in this water that will kill fish?"

You sit down to peel a potato, it turns brown in your hand while you're peeling it. It's impossible to take the skin off of a white potato without it turning brown, and yet we go to the supermarket and buy the potatoes already cut up, ready to be french fried, and they're snowy white. All you have to do is as you walk to the checkout counter, just ask the question out loud: "Now when I peel them, they turn brown . . ." Then you'll find out why theirs don't. They bleach them in formaldehyde, the same thing they embalm dead folks with.

We have 300,000 cancer deaths in this country every year because of chlorination of the water, and 150,000 deaths every year because of fluoridation of the water. Remember, I live in Massachusetts, and there is a federal law that says I cannot cross a state line and deliberately tell a lie about products that deal with interstate commerce. The cigarette industry, for some strange reason, is using a fertilizer that's so radioactive that smoking a pack and a half is equivalent to three hundred chest X-rays a day.

Somewhere I say to you, as I leave you, we have to be concerned about ourselves. We have to be concerned about this beautiful gift that we have. Somewhere we have to understand that the day you were born, you had sixty-two thousand miles of blood vessels locked in your body. If you laid your blood vessels end to end, they'd reach around this planet Earth twice with twelve thousand miles left over. And they've got you thinking some computer is a fine machine?

This system reduces us down to such insignificant nothings that you fail to realize your beauty. As a father of ten children, I feel very bad. I've never owned an automobile where I didn't check out the year, the make, the model, the down payment, the trade-in value, and when I stop and think, I put more planning into owning a jive automobile than creating God's life, then I realize something's wrong with me.

I say to you today, there's a $37 billion industry in this country for weight loss. Somewhere it's going to take discipline, and we're going to have to stop telling all these lies: "Girl, I'm not eating that much, but I'm getting so fat." Well, whatever you're eating, it's too much. And if any of you can find a way to stop eating and keep gaining weight, come see me. We can all get rich.

I close by saying to each of you that hear my voice, please get involved with physical fitness. I'm talking about you elderly folks, you women. Don't let nobody dupe you into thinking that physical fitness is just for athletes. I don't know when we're going to get past that gladiator fad. Somewhere we have to understand that this body has muscles. Your muscles must be exercised, regardless of how old you are. Organs do not have to be exercised. Sex involves organs, but we treat them like muscles. Please take care of your body. You executives, who have gone through and have forty and fifty and sixty years of brilliance in your heads, but your heart is getting ready to blow out, my God, what can you contribute to this country if you can get you another forty or fifty years with what you've already got?

Get rid of your hatred. And your racism and sexism, and all them -isms and -osms. I don't have to tell you, you're all sitting in the room, some of y'all know how you feel about Jews, and niggers, and Chicanos, and Puerto Ricans, and poor folks. I don't know why in America we keep playing games. We've got a system in this country that gives you the right to elect, but most of you don't have the right to select. We go out every four years and elect the president of the United States, but you know that doesn't count in November. It's what happens in December when the Electoral College meets. That's when they legally have the right to pick the president, and if they picked presidents like that in Russia, you'd run around talking about "that's communism for you."

You Black folks—I don't know why—all be so busy complaining about Ronald Reagan, as if everything Black folks ever wanted in life you had, and then Reagan got in and you lost it. Everybody running around, "Ronald Reagan's the president for the rich!" Like the rich were doing bad before he got there. Well, as long as America, with your funny attitudes and ways, will continue to go out and vote for the lesser of the two evils, if there's any God at all, then one day you should get the evil of the evils. Something's wrong.

Somewhere I say to you that we can make that difference. I must apologize to you white folks because we Black folks really did you all a disservice when Reagan got in. We were so busy complaining about Ronald Reagan that it took you about three months before you realized that he's really after y'all. Every time I turn on the television, I don't see anybody complaining but white folks! And I tried to tell y'all that, but y'all wouldn't listen to me! I tried to tell you when everybody was talking about the "prime" [rate], that was white folks. Most Black folks I know think prime is a rib. When he first got in and got to messing with the budget, first thing he did was cut the Coast Guard's budget by 52 percent. Remember? Now you know when Black folks wake up in the ghetto in the morning, if we don't see the Coast Guard, we're in a state of shock all day. Cut the Federal Bureau of Dams' money by 32 percent. There's one thing all Black folks know: if we go to a dance or a party, every night about ten o'clock Black folks run out and go down to the dam. You know damn well Black folks ain't got no job down at the damn dam. And last summer when Ronald Reagan signed an executive order to raise the price of yacht fuel, I cannot tell you what shock waves went through the ghetto. All summer long we discussed the high cost of yacht fuel.

I say to you today that you can make that difference. It's about getting hate out of your heart and out of your mind. That's the problem with America. We are the richest nation in the world, but we've got so much hate. Churches are closed down at nighttime. If God tried to get into church after midnight, God would be arrested for breaking and entering. So, I leave you by saying to you, you are important. You can make that difference when we cleanse out our minds. If I came here today with a pocketful of horse manure to throw on you, whose pocket stunk all day, yours or mine? If horse manure for you makes my pocket stink, then think what racism and sexism and all those -isms and -osms in your head for other people do to your mind. If I've got a choice between a stinky pocket or a stinky mind, I'll take a stinky pocket because I can get out of this coat.

So I say to you that you can make that difference. It doesn't come from all kinds of problems that we have. It's simplicity. They're talking about a Black president now. If it was me, I'd tell y'all as soon as I started to run that if you really wanted me, you better pick somebody second that you really like because if you wouldn't let me clean up this country and make this the America it should be, I'd quit. I can guarantee you that the church would lose its tax overnight. So if y'all ever see me running, don't let me in, because I'd want to know was the church in business for real estate or for souls. Then we would have that church set up where you don't have to take dictates and worry about losing something. We've got churches around here that fear everything but God. And I could guarantee y'all that the day after my inauguration, I would balance the budget. Wouldn't cost you a penny. Just using the God intelligence, we'd wipe out the Mafia, wipe out the Syndicate. Wouldn't need no army, wouldn't need no bullets, wouldn't need one cop. It's God's intelligence to take my pencil and sign an executive order that $100 bills and $50 bills will no longer be green; they'll be red. All of you that turn them in, if you don't have any income tax statement, you can burn them bills. Take that back to the Mafia, and the dope pushers, and all the illegal trillions of dollars of hustles that go on. I'm outraged living in a country with an administration that wants to tax the waitress and waiter's tips but doesn't want to get Mafia money. All you've got to do is just change the color of $100 bills, and when you bring that funny money back in from those foreign countries, you sure would have to tell me where it came from. Then we wouldn't have to worry about some poor person ripping off a food stamp. We didn't need food stamps in the first place. What we needed was nutrition stamps, and say to those of you who need it, you could only buy that which is nutritious.

So I say to you today, you can make that difference. Go to bed and get up early one morning and look at the sunrise. The sun comes out every morning and smacks nighttime clean out of the sky and never makes a sound. That's power. Ain't no power in nuclear bombs. The Russians ain't got no power. If they had some power, they could have kept Brezhnev alive. Power is not the ability to destroy whole countries. Power is the ability to build nations. Power is the ability to create love and to feed folks. That's power. And there are a whole lot of us that have that kind of power. When they drop their last nuclear bomb, we will be here. My dictates don't come from the Pentagon, or from those mad Russians. My dictates come from that God force down inside of me. If I didn't think that God force could neutralize one of these freaky nuclear bombs, then I would admit I'm praying to the wrong thing and help them pull the trigger. We have to live in a world with peace, with kindness, with honesty, with integrity. If you're not planning on doing that, then I say to you today, prepare yourself for death.

Go to bed and get up, go look at yourself in the mirror. Know what you're looking at is not only the finest thing in the universe, but it is the universe. When you can feel good about yourself, you don't have to feel bad about nobody else. One of the best ways to start feeling good about yourself is to start cleansing your body. Start being careful about what you eat. Go on a fast one day a week. Go on a long fast. When you get ready to go on a fast, they'll ask you, "Did you check with a doctor?" Well, did you check with a doctor when you started smoking? Did you check with a doctor when you snorted coke? Did you check with a doctor when you started drinking whiskey? How come everything that kills you, you don't have to check with nobody, but when you're talking about life, they want you to check with fifteen or twenty different people?

I say to you today you can make that difference. I love you. God bless you. Peace be with you. Thank you.

HARD ON THE OUTSIDE, SOFT ON THE INSIDE, BUT WILLING TO STICK HIS NECK OUT

By Christian Gregory

Dick Gregory died on August 19, 2017, at 8:40 p.m. in a beautiful, boutique hospital on the outskirts of northwest Washington, DC, a short distance from the Rock Creek Park and Potomac River trails he loved to hike.

His hiking boots swapped for wings, his soul belongs to the ancestors now. Oh, what a reunion that must've been. He'd always say to loved ones, "Call me to let me know you made it home safe. Let it ring once, then hang up. I'll know it's you." I awaited that ring. Less than forty-eight hours after his transition was the Great American Eclipse, a total solar eclipse visible across the contiguous United States from the West to the East Coasts, akin to his cross-country run. Always an inclusionist, he was a true dot connector. Dick Gregory sought out the beauty in humanity, regardless of race, religion, or creed. How befitting a tribute, an acknowledgment of his safe arrival to the ancestral plane. The eclipse, which could be observed in any part of the lower forty-eight, saw the longest period of totality (two minutes, forty seconds) across southern Illinois. Of course, this was one abundantly clear sign for the slow to perceive.

Dick Gregory, after all, was a Saluki. He attended Southern Illinois University (SIU) in Carbondale, Illinois. I could hear him in my ear: "Two minutes and 40 seconds, well that's 160 seconds. Divide that by 2 and you get 80. Now add the 4 from the 40 seconds and you get 84, exactly how old I am. See how that works?"

I smiled because Dick Gregory's numerology was never as rudimentary as my math. But for me, that was the "I've made it home safe" acknowledgment ring, and I heard it loud and clear.

Months later, while collecting, filing, and storing his possessions, I came across a small, handheld calendar in his briefcase. When I opened to the week he passed, very neatly written was "total solar eclipse" and the word *Carbondale* underlined twice. Just fascinating. He knew exactly what he was doing.

A life well-lived, yet heavily sacrificed.

Dick Gregory continued to be a leading social critic, sharing commentary and opining on matters big and small, all with his textbook smile, wit, and humor.

His annual State of the Black Union appearances became folklore: must-see TV. His brilliance and passion were the perfect formula for social media and YouTube, and his videos have garnered millions of views. He's broken through to millennials and Gen Zers, a true and honest, no-holds-barred voice of the people. His sound bites have been lifted and attached to merchandise, hats, bags, buttons, mugs, etc. I can hear him now: "When they love you, they love you."

That love sustained him in the early '90s when he returned to Washington, DC, this time taking up residence and joining his dear friend Cathy Hughes on her Radio One WOL talk show. With a daily platform, his role as a social critic blossomed. He later returned to the stage, comedy, and some occasional acting. Dick Gregory doesn't do scripts, just impromptu under the universe's direction. (This impromptu universal direction lent itself beautifully to a Kevin Durant–Nike commercial titled "The Baddest." Naturally, this is why Dick Gregory was in it.) His stand-up routine was hilarious. Not your typical old man jokes, but hilarious and witty, with stinging social commentary. The life cycle had completed its loop.

He continued his truest passion: Dick Gregory as nutritional guru. Bags full of supplements and formulations abounded. He spent hours daily in health food stores and health and wellness aisles. His 4X Formula had been developed into the Bahamian Diet and is now the Caribbean Shake for Optimal Health. Consistently on point to maximize our expression of life, Dick Gregory was a catalyst for America's healthy eating and healthy living movement.

My mother and father had been married for fifty-eight years. "Call Lil" had become a catchphrase for anyone needing to reach him. Eleven children, ten surviving, and fifteen grandchildren. Nothing ever prepares you for losing a child, and that also applies to the loss of a grandchild. I'm confident both Shayla and Bilal are laughing with and loving on Grandpa now.

In the late '90s, he survived cancer—small B-cell non-Hodgkin lymphoma. There was nothing traditional in his approach to eradicating it, yet his PET scans went from "lit up like a Christmas tree" to "nothing to see here." He enjoyed a full and total remission for the rest of his days. But honestly, did we expect anything else? In the end, it was the hunger strikes that caught up with him. He had fasted for his health, but he would routinely starve himself with hunger strikes as a form of civil disobedience. He knew at the time he was risking his life. When the body starves, it first depletes fats and carbohydrates stored throughout the body before it consumes muscle. The tunica media, the middle layer of our blood vessels, is composed of elastic and muscular tissue. My father's vascular system had systemic damage due to his hunger strikes. First were the breaches in the blood vessels in his brain—some twenty-plus cerebral strokes over a ten-year period—and finally the breach of his aortic arch, the largest artery in the human body. It was this breach that proved to be fatal. Chronologically eighty-four, but biologically more like 104, his body, mind, and soul had a lot of miles.

As he began his eighty-fourth revolution around the sun, he voiced both delight and continued concern for the plight of humanity. It never mattered much to him if the glass was half full or half empty. Either way, it was refillable, and he was always eager to fill it up with clean water. If the glass represents love, then his glass runneth over.

For the final years of his life, he kept a hand tally counter in his pocket. For hours he'd simply click it like a hyperactive child with a fidget spinner. He looked so peaceful; I'd look on and smile. Some time went by before I asked him what he was doing. He said he was clicking every time he said, "Thank you, God." He went on to say that at times his life felt unreal and he was beyond grateful. When someone would say "How are you, Brother Dick?" he'd say, "Fantastic, and getting better."

The week he passed was filled with laughter and phone calls in a large, beautiful room that felt more like a hotel suite than a hospital room. Flowers from all over the world poured in. It felt like a botanical garden. The smell of fresh flowers hit you the moment the elevator door opened. The family remained by his side, on vigil, to immediately address his every wish or desire. He wasn't in pain but certainly wasn't his normal self. He was in constant and very deep reflection, occasionally asking about a friend he hadn't mentioned in decades. One night he began talking to his brother Presley. Presley had died years ago. Occasionally, he'd whisper in my ear, "Hey, Doc, this definitely is not what they think this is."

I hadn't worried too much about his talking to folks not in the room, or his gut feeling about what was amiss. He had an infection that had elevated his white blood cells. For every white blood cell present, there's one less red blood cell, which creates a form of hypoxia. And hypoxia exacerbates age-related dementia, sometimes alarmingly so. I focused more on logging on to the hospital's portal and reviewing his daily lab results. They ebbed and flowed without medical logic. His team was a bit baffled but undeterred and unwilling to release him until his medical mystery was solved. It was day seven in the hospital when the astute eye of a radiologist, reviewing the films remotely, discovered what we quickly realized was a major medical problem. My mother and siblings surrounded my father and held and kissed him. It wasn't long before things deteriorated.

He wasn't in pain; he smiled and winked a lot. Oddly enough, he seemed relieved to have been right, almost an "I told you I ain't crazy." He knew what no one else did; he went out on his own terms. Lord knows he'd earned that.

The next few months literally went by in a blur. I spent over twelve hours in the church the day of my father's funeral. His service was seven hours long. I'm clear he would have objected to that. But funerals are for the closure of everyone you leave behind. There was a lot of closure that day. Newspapers around the world paid wonderful tributes to a life so profoundly well lived. There was a litany of headlines from across the globe. I've never seen the words *justice* and *activist* used so many times. The *New York Times* said Dick Gregory was a "sledgehammer for justice." I'm certain he'd smile on that one.

Almost five years later, I reflect often. Freedom is never free. The heavy price and toll of a life of service will always catch up to you. I'm positive my father wouldn't have changed a thing. Life was hard back then, especially hard on Black people. My father's mother, Lucille, died in her forties, and his father, Presley, died at sixty-five. Even with all the scars of extreme sacrifice, Dick Gregory long outlived his genetics.

Once an adult, twice a child. We were determined that Dick Gregory's second childhood would make up for all of the shortcomings of his first. Laughter, security, comfort, family, friends, and love were omnipresent.

Gone but never forgotten, he not only cemented his legacy but planted seeds of wisdom and knowledge everywhere. His message today is as vital as ever. His books, albums, and lectures are chopped and stored by metadata, instantly accessible and streaming through digital devices throughout the world. He's in the universal matrix sounding the alarm. His original memoir has now been released in Japan and Croatia, and as of this writing, he's currently trending in Indonesia. His entire book catalog is being republished, with six titles refreshed as trade paperbacks and now available as e-books and audiobooks. I foresee a future with countless biographies, stage plays, and film and television projects—each one trying to capture this difficult-to-define man. His work is far from done. In a sense, it's only just begun.

CREDITS

PART I: THE BODY (1932–1960)

The bulk of the material in Part I—Excerpted from notes and transcripts, in addition to audio recordings made by Robert Lipsyte between September 1963 and February 1964, reproduced by permission from Robert Lipsyte and Gregory Estate.

Breakthrough—Interview with Mike Wallace: Reproduced from Mike Wallace Papers, Syracuse University, https://library.syr.edu/digital/guides/w/wallace_m.htm.

Breakthrough—Interview with Paul Krassner: Reproduced from "An Impolite Interview with Dick Gregory," *The Realist*, no. 29 (September 1961), http://ep.tc /realist/29/index.html.

PART II: THE MIND (1961–1970)

Congressional Testimony: Reproduced from *Investigation of Discrimination Patterns in the Performing Arts* (Washington, DC: US Government Printing Office, 1963), https://www.google.com/books/edition/Employment_Practices_in_the _Performing_A/X-mbkSK2Sp4C?hl=en.

Interview with Ralph Gleason: Reproduced from "Ralph Gleason Interviewing Dick Gregory," KPFA, aired June 23, 1963, American Archive of Public Broadcasting, https://americanarchive.org/catalog/cpb-aacip_28-k649p2wm6m.

Selma Speeches—Brown Chapel AME Church: Reproduced by permission from the Gregory Estate.

Freedom Summer: Reproduced from "Mississippi Eyewitness," Special Issue, *Ramparts*, 1964, https://dickatlee.com/issues/mississippi/mississippi_eyewitness /mississippi_eye witness_full.html#dickg.

Interview with Larry Wilde: Reproduced from Larry Wilde, *Great Comedians Talk About Comedy* (New York: New York Laugh.com, 1968).

Malcolm: Reproduced by permission from the Gregory Estate.

Speech at Vietnam Day: Reproduced by permission from the Gregory Estate. *Berkeley Teach-In: Vietnam*, Folkways Records, liner notes, https://media .smithsonianfolkways.org/liner_notes/folkways/FW05765.pdf.

Martin: Reproduced by permission from the Gregory Estate.

COINTELPRO: Reproduced from FBI documents; Rob Warden, "FBI Memo: Use Mob Against Dick Gregory," *Chicago Tribune*, March 10, 1978.

Write Me In: Reproduced by permission from the Gregory Estate. Dick Gregory (with Shelia P. Moses), *Callus on My Soul* (Atlanta: Longstreet Press, 2000), 124–25, 165–66.

Imagine: Reproduced by permission from the Gregory Estate. "Bed Peace Starring John Lennon & Yoko Ono (1969)," YouTube, https://youtu.be/mRjjiOV 003Q?t=1044.

PART III: THE SPIRIT (1971–2017)

My Answer to Genocide: Reproduced by permission from Dick Gregory, "My Answer to Genocide," *EBONY*, October 1971.

The Circuit: Reproduced by permission from the Gregory Estate. "Dick Gregory speaking at UCLA, 1/27/1972," YouTube, https://www.youtube.com/watch?v=CAZDuMQFdmc.

From Stand-Up Comic to Lie-Down Martyr: Reproduced from Roger M. Williams, "From Stand-Up Comic to Lie-Down Martyr," *World*, August 15, 1972.

Caught in the Act: Reproduced by permission from the Gregory Estate. *Caught in the Act* (United Artists).

The JFK Investigation: Permission from Steve Jaffe/Jaffe & Company. Reproduced from *Good Night America*, ABC Television, March 6, 1975.

A Winning Formula: Reproduced by permission from the Dick Gregory and Christian Gregory, *The 12 Essentials for Optimal Health* (Chicago: Wellness In Nature, 2021).

Amandla Festival: Reproduced by permission from the Gregory Estate. Amandla Production Collective and Haymarket Concerts, https://www.youtube.com/watch?v=xNXz3NIi7FE.

Iran Hostage Crisis: Reproduced by permission from the Gregory Estate. "Dick Gregory," WGBH, September 9, 1980, Boston TV News Digital Library, http://bostonlocaltv.org/catalog/V_763I2PXVICLK17B.

Pilgrim in Search of Liberation: Reproduced by permission from "Dick Gregory: Pilgrim in Search of Liberation," *Message*, March/April 1981.

"Something Must Be Wrong": Reproduced by permission from the Gregory Estate. "Dick Gregory 3.18.1983," YouTube, https://www.youtube.com/watch?v=Id7cL sUHE5Y.

ACKNOWLEDGMENTS

Heartfelt gratitude and appreciation to everyone who facilitated the historical undertakings of Dick Gregory's literary endeavors.

Specifically, I'd like to acknowledge the folks who made this Herculean scope scalable. An embarrassment of riches in content whittled down and presented in this succinct linear literary work was profoundly difficult yet exhilarating. This project would've been unfathomable without the support of so many. Profound gratitude to *The Essential Dick Gregory* village and everyone who has supported and uplifted the Estate of Dick Gregory.

With love and appreciation, Christian

Lil and the family: Dick Gregory was the patriarch of his family, a father to the movement and a Baba to his people. I'd like to thank and lift up his nuclear family, his answer to genocide, and the wind beneath his wings. No one was a more sustaining up-current than the love of his life, spouse extraordinaire, business partner, and best friend, Lil. Lillian Gregory, and the **Gregory children** Michele, Lynne, Richard Jr. (d), Satori (Pamela), Paula, Zenobia (Stephanie), Gregory, Miss, Christian, Ayanna, and Yohance. **Grands/ Greatgrands:** Shayla, Joshua, Julian, Olivia, Sikani, Afrika, Eusi, Zenzele, Busara, Bilal, Naima, Kalim, Dawnesha, Odeama,

Tayshaun, Naomi, Everest, Raquawn, Kali, Tierea, Ahmani, Jayce, Hodori, Leon, Auria, Zion, Ava, Titus, Busayo, Bodhi, Zolani, Akoma, and Tumelo. **Dick Gregory's mother and siblings:** Lucille, Presley, Delores, Garland, Pauline, and Ronald.

Amistad at HarperCollins Publishers: Tracy Sherrod, Jennifer Baker, Francesca Walker, Ashley Yepsen, Maya Lewis, Brieana Garcia, Tara Parsons, Judith Curr, and the collective HC team. What a blessing.

This publishing partnership began with Dick Gregory and continues with his estate. This is the fifth active publication with additional republications in the pipeline. We are grateful beyond words and measure for this partnership and the campaign to stamp out ignorance while lifting up humanity. Information is power, and our partnership's collective power is immeasurable.

Serendipity Literary Agency: The official literary agency for the Estate of Dick Gregory. Thank you Regina Brooks, for your vision and mastery of your sector. You were the spark that put this project in motion. Here's to what's next.

Melissa Fernandez: It takes a village and successful villages need wise leadership. Thank you for your brilliance and your perfectionism. This certainly wasn't easy but you lightened the load every step of the way. Our journey continues to be an honor and a blessing. Love you to life.

Professor Edward Schmitt: What is any project without structure? This assignment was massive, ambitious beyond belief. Impossible at first glance to get one's arms around. Ed was our structural engineer with an understanding of our subject that can only come from a tremendous amount of research balanced with love and admiration. Heartfelt gratitude and appreciation to my 1970 brethren. Thank you for your intellect and acumen.

Robert Lipsyte: A significant amount of material that comprised this project was recorded in 1963 by Robert Lipsyte. Robert and Dick talked for hours at a time all while classical music played in the background. A young, thirty-one-year-old Dick Gregory, laser focused and highly opinionated, would unpack issues with great depth and clarity. Thank you to the Lipsyte family for gatekeeping and protecting what is now one of the estate's most prized collections. Bob, thank you for your passion, professionalism, integrity, vision, and most important, being an amazing friend to Dick Gregory.

Literary Collaborators (present and past): Alvin (Ferdy) Banks, John Bellamy, Mathieu Bitton, Gregory Carr, Melissa Fernandez, Dr. Alvenia Fulton, Andre Gaines, Steve Jaffe, Mark Lane, Robert Lipsyte, Jertha Love, James R. McGraw, Joe Morton, Shelia Moses, Kristine Noble, Imani Noble, James Sanders, Edward Schmitt, Nancy Sheppard, Jodie Shull, Martha Smith, Clifford Thompson, Alarra Tozin, Mike Watley, Dr. E. Faye Williams, Cheryl Woodruff, Jefry Andres Wright, Emma Young.

Friends and Partners: Ava-Mae, Juanita Moore Akita, Todd Albertson, Angela D. Alsobrooks, Mark Bair, Rushern Baker, Christopher Barkley, Rev. Michael Beckwith, Dr. Mahin Banou Beiraghdar, Harry Belafonte, John Bellamy, Free Benjamin, Muriel Bowser, Barron Preston (BP), Juanita Britton, Gordon Brooks, Darryl Brooks, Jesse Buggs, Nick Buggs, Jack Canfield, Nick Cannon, John Carlin, Dave Chappelle, Lena Chase, Michael Colyer, Tommy Davidson, Quiana Davis, Guadalís Del Carmen, Michael J. Dennis, Annette d'Epagnier, Annette Dreher, Michael Eric Dyson, Valerie Edwards, Joni Eisenberg, Glenn Ellis, Tanee Elston, Reena Evers, Anna Fernandez, Melissa Fernandez, Nathaniel Gaither, Mark Gallardo, Shaunte Gates, Edwin Lee Gibson, Katie Green,

Mark Gregory, Diana Gregory, Saleem Gyau, Roy and Betty Hamlin, Calvin Hawkins II, Alison Henderson, Ron Herd, Cheo Hurley, Bernard Jackson, James Kelly, Martin Luther King III, Bernice King, Gretchen Law, Zoe Leigh, Stephanie Lipscomb, Breta London, Peter Lopes, George Lopez, Joe and Sherry Madison, Molly McCluskey, James McKinney, Killer Mike, Sidney Miller, Marilyn Milloy, Arya Mohsen, Niki Moore, Mark Anthony Neal, Lee Nelson, Janice Nesmith, Cinque Northern, Dr. Jyonna Norwood, Lawrence O'Donnell, Whitney Nolan Parker, Shirin Parsa, Shabnam Parsa, Demont Pinder, Mark Poitras, Rain Pryor, Art Rocker, John Gould Rubin, John Salley, Rob Schneider, Gerald Scott, Ilyasah Shabazz, Andy Shallal, Renee Shareef, Keith Silver, Cheryl Smith, Ivan D. Smith, Sara Soulati, Daryl Spivey, Arthur Thomas, Daniel Thomas, Mark Thomashow, Roland Martin, Mark Thompson, Reggie Toran, Chris Tucker, Cicely Tyson, Iyanla Vanzant, Martina Washington, Joan Wilbon, Dr. E. Faye Williams, Rodney Williams, Andrew Wyatt, Maimouna Youssef.

Organizational Friends and Partners: Attorney Ricky Anderson, Audible, Ben's Chili Bowl (Virginia Ali & family), Black Magic Entertainment (Art Martin), Bronner Bros., Cinemation Studios (Andre Gaines), City of Praise (Bishop Joel & Pastor Ylawnda Peebles, Payton Wynne, Canute Ellis), Clarke & Associates (Priscilla Clarke, Chef Huda, Mark Clarke, Qasim Clarke), Congressional Black Caucus, GreiBO Gravity (Davis Grei), HartBeat Productions (Kevin Hart, Bryan Smiley), Hillman Grad Productions (Lena Waithe, Rishi Rajani, ~TOAODG Album~, Danni Baylor, Cory Henry, Lupe Fiasco, Big K.R.I.T., Uno Hype, Saint Bodhi, Statik Selektah, Talib Kweli, Haile Supreme, A Room Full of Mirrors, Terrace Martin, BJ The Chicago Kid, Bobby Sessions, Maxo, Black Thought, Tebbs Maqubela, Kyle Townsend), ICM

(Lorrie Bartlett, Alicia Gordon, Daniel Kirschen), Maandi House Entertainment (Wesley Snipes), National Association for Equal Opportunity in Higher Education (Lezli Baskerville), National Congress of Black Women (Dr. E. Faye Williams), Smithsonian Institute—National Museum of African American History & Culture (Kinshasha Holman Conwill), Ncredible Entertainment (Nick Cannon), Schomburg Center for Research in Black Culture (Joy Bivens), SimonSays Entertainment (Ron Simons), Solid Photography (Ron Baker), Stein Sperling (David De Jong, Steven Widdes), Tash Moseley Management, The Guzman Law Group (Denise Guzman and Carol Contes), The Law Office of Rosalind Ray, The Rabin Group (Robert Rabin), Tower Hill Farm Entertainment, UrbanOne (Cathy Hughes), WPFW (Katea Stitt, Jerry Paris), Word Collections (Jeff Price).

EDITORIAL AND RESEARCH TEAM

ABOUT THE AUTHOR AND EDITOR

Richard "Dick" Claxton Gregory was a comedian, civil rights activist, and cultural icon who first performed in public in the 1950s. He is on Comedy Central's list of "100 Greatest Standups" and was the author of sixteen books, with millions of copies sold. While working as an entertainer, he was known for being outspoken about social change and starting a healthy clean-eating campaign.

Dr. Christian Claxton Gregory is the eighth child of Dick and Lillian Gregory. Born in Chicago, he was raised on a 1,000 acre farm in Plymouth, Massachusetts, where the pastoral setting and lifelong lessons in wellness spurred his interest in physiology and the mind-body connection. After graduating from Morgan State University, he earned a doctor of chiropractic degree from Life University in Atlanta. Dr. Gregory practiced in Washington for twenty-five years, caring for DC natives, leading entertainment figures, and friends in the movement, including Rosa Parks, Coretta Scott King, Betty Shabazz, Dorothy Height, Cicely Tyson, and Stevie Wonder. When Dick Gregory decided to resume an active speaking and entertainment schedule, he became his father's manager. Together they formed Dick Gregory Media, Inc. in 2015. Dr.

Gregory's unique combined experiences in patient care and entertainment management fostered the desire to develop the linkages between activism, communication, the performing arts, and physical well-being. To that end, he established Tower Hill Farm Health & Wellness and Tower Hill Farm Entertainment. Since his passing in 2017, Christian Gregory has managed his father's estate and intellectual property, and has successfully guided the development of other projects about his father's life, including the stage play *Turn Me Loose* and the film *The One and Only Dick Gregory*.